THE BEAUTY OF *Hope*

THE BEAUTY
OF *Hope*

KIMBERLY BALDWIN

XULON PRESS

Xulon Press
2301 Lucien Way #415
Maitland, FL 32751
407.339.4217
www.xulonpress.com

Printed in the United States of America.

ISBN-13: 978-1-6628-0494-6
Ebook: 978-1-6628-0495-3

DEDICATION

To the: Miranda family. Thank you for sharing the love of Jesus with me. I am forever grateful for you.

TABLE OF CONTENTS

ACKNOWLEDGMENTS

The Miranda family – Thank you for loving me with the love of Jesus. I am forever changed for the better because of you.

Brad and Cari Stanhope – Thank you for the invaluable gift of spending your precious time reading and editing my first book. I thank God for you.

Xulon Press – Thank you for helping me navigate the waters of publishing my first book. Your guidance, wisdom, and help will ever be appreciated.

Pastor Joe and Teena Skiles – Thank you for the way you shepherd New Hope Church. It is an honor, joy, and delight to be under your leadership for such a time as this. I love and treasure you both.

Mom and Dad – Thank you for your decades of hard work. Thank you for staying together for my benefit. Thank you for loving me.

Janelle, Evan, and Bella – You are the arrows in my quiver, and I am beyond blessed to be your mom. I pray Jesus takes you further than you can imagine. His plans for you are great, and I am honored to partner with Daddy and Jesus to launch you into the world. Thank you for allowing me to share parts of your story.

My husband, John – You will forever be God's gift to me. Thank you for loving me always, being my best friend, and following Jesus. I love you dearly.

BEGINNING

Hello, beloved of God! My name is Kimberly and I love writing. When I was growing up, I wanted to be a wife, a mom, and a teacher (I loved playing school with my dolls). The wife and mom part played out, but I never became a teacher. My journey through life, thus far, has been filled with its fair share of ups and downs. For the longest time, I saw the downs more than the ups. I used to say, "If I write a book one day, it will be called *Hopes Dashed*." In my mid-30s, Jesus changed my perspective. I was in the middle of my third pregnancy, and it was a difficult and challenging time.

Discouragement was knocking fiercely at my heart's door, and I felt it would break the door down by force. As I faced that season clinging to Jesus and the faith I placed in Him I was desperate for encouragement. Daily feelings of despair screamed that this pregnancy would turn out to be yet another dashed hope. All I had was my faith and the Word of God, which stands forever. After a heartbreaking report from the doctors, I went straight home and called my mom. When things are hard, we all long for someone to just hold us and tell us it will be okay. Mom was in California, and I was in New Jersey. In lieu of a hug, I made a phone call. As Mom prayed with me, I could feel a peace flood my heart. I still didn't know how things would turn out, but I was encouraged and that brought a hope to carry on. It was then that I was reminded of another phone call to Mom—one where she spoke to me and a shift happened in my soul. She said something to the effect of, "When you write that book of yours, I ask that Jesus would give you a different title and change your heart about hopes being dashed."

After our phone call, I turned to the Bible, and Jesus had me land on Psalm 119. Being the longest of the Psalms, it felt a little daunting, but then I stumbled upon verse 116.

Sustain me, my God, according to your promises, and I will live; do not let my hopes be dashed. Psalm 119:116 NIV

These words were penned before I was ever a thought in my parents' minds. I'd read them before, but at this moment, I finally saw it and I was blown away. The story of my life started to change. Jesus brought a new perspective, and His truth started to shift the way I saw everything. At that moment, I knew that Jesus gave me a new title for my book—*The Beauty of Hope*. Instead of looking at every challenging circumstance as if it would be the end of me, I chose to stand on His Word and live according to His promises.

It hasn't been easy, but Jesus gives us a hope to carry on. Life will always be filled with mountains and valleys. There will be life and there will be death. Jesus even made it a point to let His followers know that hard times would come.

I have told you all this so that you may have peace in me. Here on earth you will have many trials and sorrows. But take heart, because I have overcome the world.
John 16:33

So I chose to take heart, because there is One who has overcome. When I was an infant, my life was saved by our very own Fireman Angel (you'll read about him soon). I didn't know that truth until someone told me the story. Our stories, our testimonies, are powerful.

They triumphed over him by the blood of the Lamb and by the word of their testimony.
Revelation 12:11a NIV

This book is filled with my stories, and it's all for His glory. As I thought about the chapter titles, the reminder of my original title, *Hopes Dashed,* came to me. Jesus spoke sweetly to my heart and told me that each chapter should have the word *Hope* followed by a dash and then the word that He gave me through each testimony you will read. These words are things in which I hope and things in which I am destined to walk as His Beloved. Dear one, they are meant for you as well. I pray that as you read these pages, Jesus will give you such a deep well of hope that it carries you through anything that comes your way. Join me as I tell of how Jesus changed my perspective and delivered the beauty of hope in His perfect timing.

Chapter 1

HOPE-LIGHT

D arkness. Before there was light, everything was dark. Growing up, my childhood was filled with darkness. Isn't that how it is for all of us? In the secret place of our mother's womb, surrounded by darkness, we begin to form. A piece of our mother and a piece of our father collide, and we begin. I believe life begins at conception.

My earliest memory of life was being left in a dark room. I was an infant and one of my parents placed me in my crib. I vividly remember someone walking away and turning off the light in my room. My parents' silhouettes were visible in the doorway as the hall light spilled its brilliance into the room. The next thing I see are my little hands as they pull a foot toward my mouth. Years later, I would be told the story of how I used to suck my toes as an infant. I laughed about it. However, there was no mistaking the mark of darkness I felt imprinted on my little life.

At some point during my infancy, a huge amount of light spread its way into our lives in the form of a fire. Mom was working long days at a restaurant and was exhausted with a new baby. Relieved of her shift early and sent home to get some much-needed rest, she did the exact opposite. As most moms do, once she settled me for a nap, she chose work over rest. The car was just too dirty, and this stubborn Missourian decided to "warsh" the car. With her long brown hair pinned up in her usual bun, she got to work. Once the work was completed and her cigarette put out, Mom finally sat down to relax. Sometime later, a knock at the door woke her. A man she never saw before informed her that the garage was on fire. Apparently, while vacuuming the car, she also managed to suck up some hot cigarette butts. The man told Mom he would get the hose and she grabbed me and headed across the street to the neighbor's house to call 911. The fire crew came and put out the flames, which thankfully only burned the garage. As she stood there, it hit her: Mom needed to find the man who saved our lives. He was nowhere to be found. We call him our Fireman Angel.

As a young girl, my parents both relied a bit too much on the bottle—not when it came to feeding me. They were both alcoholics. Dad hid his habit most days. He put long, stressful hours in at a grocery store as a butcher and meat manager. He was my mom's tall, dark, and handsome, until they separated. Mom's days were long and stressful as well. She was known to be a drunk who dabbled in other addictions. When I was three years old, their marriage faced what anyone would think would be its final chapter. Divorce decrees were declared, and the darkness seemed to thicken.

For a while, I would go back and forth between parents like a ping-pong ball bouncing between two people who were being a bit too hard on themselves and each other. Mom had friends and would stay with them at what I used to call the party house. Except for me, it was a pretty scary party. While some memories can be fuzzy, what is clear is that Mom and her friends would be loud and drunk, and the smell of marijuana gave me a headache. I would hide in a back room with my favorite dolly and pray the dog who lived at the house wouldn't come and bite me. So many fears surrounded me, but there was a Light with me all along. It just took a while for me to see it.

One of the most brilliant lights on this side of heaven came to us with the entrance of the Miranda family into our lives. Mrs. Loretta Miranda, a sweet, loving pastor's wife was my babysitter from about six months until I turned nine. Light seemed to flood their home. Their home was an example of what a home should really be. While my parents bounced me back and forth for a while, I always had this little sanctuary in the middle of it. The Miranda household was a treasured spot of love and safety for my young heart.

I am not sure how long it was after the divorce when my parents came to an olive branch agreement. Mom moved back in with Dad in order to shelter me from the horrors of being tossed between the two of them. However, marriage wasn't an option. As stubborn as my Missourian mom can be, my Portuguese dad tops her, hands down. When they divorced, Dad declared he would never take Mom back. So, an agreement of sorts was set, and Mom moved into one of the spare bedrooms, while Dad slept in the master—together, yet separate. It was confusing for me to have both parents home again but not married. While we ate meals, watched TV, and even went on trips together, Mom and Dad were not together, and it broke my heart.

Occasionally, Mom and Dad would get into arguments and a deep sadness darkened my heart all the more. Those times were really scary. An adventure to find a quiet place was in order. Gathering all the keys in the house I could find, my dolly and I would sneak out and sit in one of the cars with doors locked, pretending we were driving away from it all. Usually, I would sneak back inside without them even noticing. On one occasion, Dad came looking for me, and in that moment, I felt a bit of rescue and protection in the midst of the darkness. However, we never talked about anything that was going on. I just wanted answers. I wanted to know that my parents were okay and that Mom wouldn't be taking any more of her long naps after drinking from the big bottle. It was as if Mom was sick, and I just wanted her to be better. I wanted my parents to get married again and have the security of their bond of love. I just wanted a little light in the darkness.

Sometime when I was five, that little light started to shine. I remember spending more and more time with the Miranda family. Mom and Dad worked hard to provide for our broken-up family. Dad would drop me off in the early morning hours on his way to work, and I remember being passed from his arms to Loretta's, then gently laid in a bed to finish my night's sleep. Loretta, my babysitter, and her husband, Jerry, and their children became like a second family to me. Meals at the Miranda's house weren't started until Jesus was properly thanked. Days were filled with laughter and fun with the other children Loretta watched in her home daycare. Often being the last child to leave for the day, I remember the sweet devotional times they would have after dinner. The Bible would be open, maybe we would sing a song, and prayer time was a must. The Mirandas had three children, and they were like older siblings to me. They spent time with me and gave me a love for board games. I will never forget the time when one of Loretta's daughters had so many children in the game of Life that she had to get a second car. Light was cascading into my darkness.

Loretta was always pouring encouraging words into me. She spoke about Jesus often. To this day, I can hear her saying, "Kimmy, you are so special, and Jesus loves you very much." It was the warmth of her kindness and the glow in her eyes that drew me to the love of Jesus. Loretta and her family welcomed me as one of their own. Often, I would be there over the weekend and attend church with them on Sundays, midweek service on Wednesday nights, and in the summer, there was church camp and VBS, also known as Vacation Bible School.

Sunday school was always a highlight of the week for me. I loved seeing the Bible stories come to life on the felt board! For those too young to know what a felt board is, well, let's just say you missed out. Little felt Bible characters, props, animals, and scenery were stuck to a felt board. It was all the rage in the 1980s for Sunday school teachers. The best part was getting chosen to place a Bible character on the board. It was like you were jumping into the story, and the Bible came alive to my little heart. One time during a church service, I felt the love of Jesus so strongly that by the time the altar call was given, I was running to the altar, pouring out my tears. At the tender age of five, I asked Jesus to be my Lord and Savior and live in my heart forever. The Light of the world was now living in me.

Jesus changes everything and at the same time everything didn't change. His light can both expose and brighten. At times, it's blinding and yet it is also a warm and gentle glow. I found "this little light of mine," but I wasn't able to see how His light was shining in my darkness. I felt safe knowing Jesus loved me. However, things at home were still the same. Mom was still smoking like a chimney and turning to the bottle for escape. There were even times when she would offer liquor to me in the bottle cap. My quiet, bold response would always be to quote Psalm 118:24: "This is the day the Lord has made. We will rejoice and be glad in it." I would then return quietly to my room, keep to myself, and play Sunday school with my dolls, sharing the light with them, even though things were still so dark. I was determined to save every last one of those dolls!

At some point, Mom went to AA and gave up drinking and drugs for good. She asked Dad to not bring any alcohol into the house, and so he hid his in shadowed places—the garage, the water tank of the toilet, tucked under the bathroom sink, you name it. He was desperate and couldn't give up drinking as Mom had done. Her light started to shine and a peace started to rest on us. I was getting older and started noticing just how much Dad was drinking—mostly on Sundays after golfing. Mom saw the Light and gave her heart to Jesus. We started attending church together every week, which was an answer to my prayers. Dad, however, chose to spend his Sundays on the golf course. I remember him once mentioning a road sign that gave him a laugh. On the sign were two arrows, one pointing right and the other left. It said, "Play or Pray." While we were praying, he was often playing golf and then drinking a round with his buddies. Sundays were also family dinner nights at my paternal grandparent's house. After golf, Dad would come home and we all jumped into the car and off to Grandma's we went. My grandparents spoke mostly Portuguese and since I didn't, I was often at a loss as to what was going on. However, Sundays were full of family and food, as well as fear.

Grandpa loved his wine and enjoyed making his own toxic concoction in the shed out back behind their house. And boy, do I mean toxic. I remember that shed door opening while I was playing with cousins in the backyard and my eyes would start to water. It was some strong stuff, to say the least. My dad is one of ten children—nine boys and one girl. We all packed into Grandma and Grandpa's tiny, two-bedroom home just about every Sunday evening of my childhood. The cousins would be playing, the moms would join Grandma in the kitchen to prepare a meal, and the men would drink beer and wine while smoking in the backyard. Grandma was another one of those points of light in my childhood. She was a simple woman but loved her family with all she was. Her loving hugs brought comfort. Her hospitality was supreme. Her little chocolate and vanilla ice cream cups were a bit of heaven on a wooden spoon. I may not have been able to understand her broken English all the time, but I sure loved playing double solitaire with her and laughing as she cheered for the sumo wrestlers on TV.

On more than one occasion, the uncles would be so drunk, a fight would break out. Sometimes Grandpa would yell at Grandma, but they always put up with each other. One night the uncles were fighting so bad that the cops showed up. I thought we were all going to jail, but I don't believe anyone actually did. What did happen was a strict warning from the police officer that my dad should, under no circumstances, drive home that night. Mom took the keys and for the first time made the forty-five-minute drive back home in the dark. Dad was sitting in the backseat and fear clawed at my heart.

Fear caused me to keep to myself. I prayed and prayed for so long, and Mom was finally better from her drinking disease. However, now I was starting to see how much Dad struggled. In my teen years, family dinners didn't happen as often. Cousins were growing up and starting families of their own, and we just weren't getting together like we used to. It was the end of an era.

Sundays became a worrying night. The Miranda family moved several hours away to take a pastoral job. With them leaving, somehow we just stopped going to church. It left a huge void in my life. I missed them so much, but they gave me Jesus and I was so very thankful for that. To this day, though miles are between us, they are still part of my family. So, Sundays became quiet and worrisome. Dad was playing golf longer and coming home later and later. There were nights I would go to sleep and not know if he would ever come home. It was so scary. I didn't know what he was doing, where he was, or if he would make it home safely. One night, in my teen years, I was just so fed up with the worry that I decided to go for a drive. It was dark and I was a new driver, so I planned on driving around the neighborhood a few times just to clear my head. The neighborhood clubhouse was coming into view, and parked right in front of it was my Dad's truck with the camper shell on it. I was paralyzed but drove up and parked to see what he was doing. I found him lying down in the back of his truck sleeping off his liquor. I didn't know why he would come so close and yet not come home. Maybe he felt the need to sleep it off so he wouldn't discourage Mom in her sobriety. Whatever his reasons, it made me angry and fearful and heartbroken all at the same time. It also laid another brick in the foundational resolve of my life. The resolve that I would never touch drugs, cigarettes, or alcohol, because it had the power to bring destruction to a person and their loved ones.

The dark days of childhood blurred into the past, but it was always there, never really too far behind me. What happens to us as children can leave serious marks on our hearts and souls. What we often don't have at the time is perspective, which is so valuable. Years later, in my thirties, the hope of light crashed into my life. At the time, I was living in New Jersey, a long way off from my hometown of Concord, California. I was married with two children at the time and still loving Jesus. I went up for prayer one evening during a leadership retreat with our church. I was longing for more of Jesus, but deep down I really had a question. Why was it so dark? I knew Jesus for so long, yet when I would think back on those childhood moments, they felt so dark. I knew Jesus loved me and I had faith. Jesus is a kind gentleman, and He will give us what we need when we need it. What I really needed was perspective, and as someone prayed over me I got just that.

While the woman at the altar prayed over my life, for more of Jesus, I saw an image of myself as a little girl. I was holding my favorite dolly and we were hiding in the room at the party house. Then, as if it was a moving picture panning out, the scene got larger and I saw the true reality of the darkness. Surrounding me were three very tall angels. They had huge wings that rose about two feet above their heads and went all the way to the ground. Each angel was holding a shield and a glittering sword. Their backs were toward me and they were on watch, guarding me. At that moment, I heard Jesus whisper to my soul, "My child, it is always darkest under the shadow of my wings." The tears began to flow...years of heartache and questioning and feeling alone in the darkness started to wash away.

While I faced many things that were never meant for a child to see, the reality was that God's hand was on my life from the very beginning. So, I am learning some perspective. His light is illuminating what I cannot see. He began taking the dark moments of the past to reveal the light of His truth. A new sense of security flooded my soul. The Word of God says some amazing things, and these are truths He brought to my soul that night.

He will cover you with his feathers. He will shelter you with his wings. His faithful promises are your armor and protection.
Psalm 91:4

Those who live in shelter of the Most High will find rest in the shadow of the Almighty.
Psalm 91:1

Have mercy on me, O God, have mercy! I look to you for protection. I will hide beneath the shadow of your wings until the danger passes by.
Psalm 57:1

How precious is your unfailing love, O God! All humanity finds shelter in the shadow of your wings.
Psalm 36:7

Let me live forever in your sanctuary, safe beneath the shelter of your wings!
Psalm 61:4

Because you are my helper, I sing for joy in the shadow of your wings.
Psalm 63:7

These Psalms mean so much to me. They are a healing balm to the darkness of my childhood. They remind me that His light is not affected by darkness—it shines on strongly. His shadow is a place of safety. So many times in the Bible, when an angel comes to deliver a message, the people respond with fear. In just about every account, the angel will respond with a few powerful words, "Fear not," or "Be not afraid." Sometimes the scariest moments in our lives only feel that way because a host of angels is surrounding us.

In the New Testament, there is a different version of being tucked under a set of wings. In Matthew 23:37, Jesus says, *"O Jerusalem, Jerusalem, the city that kills the prophets and stones God's messengers! How often I have wanted to gather your children together as a hen protects her chicks beneath her wings, but you wouldn't let me."*

Now, this verse is not implying that we are fearful little chickens, but then again, aren't we? So often, we respond in fear to life's circumstances. As a little chicken, if you want to stay away from danger, you have to stay close to the mother hen. When danger does come her way, she is unable to run around the whole farmyard and gather every single one of her chicks. She will be able to gather only those who are close to her. The lesson here is that we need to stay close to the Father, Son, and Holy Spirit in order to be safe. When we are like chicks who are gathered up under His wings, not only is it dark, but it's going to get hot. It may be hard to breathe, and you will likely feel hard-pressed. But God has you in the shadow, a place of safety and security. Is there any other place one should desire more to be? No matter what you are facing in this life, know that there is a divine protection detail on your case. It may not be what you think it should be at the moment, but God is faithful to watch over those He loves, and He loves you very much! Things are not always what they seem, and there is always more going on than what we see with our natural eyes.

Now, about that darkness in our beginning. Do you know what happens in the hidden darkness of our mother's womb? An amazing discovery was made in 2016 regarding conception. Scientists were able to capture a video of a burst of light when the sperm penetrates the egg. It has to do with some kind of zinc firework causing light to shine in the darkness of the womb.[1] There are those who will say

---

[1]   Paul, "Radiant Zinc Fireworks."

it's just a reaction of chemicals, but I find it amazing that while we are formed in the darkness, it all starts with a flash of light. Even before our eyes could see, a brightness flooded our lives. Beloved, remember that on the darker days of life. You were created so God's face could shine upon you, and so you could shine with the Light of Heaven. Let your soul run free with the hope of light.

Chapter 2

HOPE-LOVE

lone. Each one of us has felt alone at some point in our lives. For a very long time, at the core of who I am, I have felt alone. Maybe it was partly due to being an only child. How I longed to have siblings, especially an older brother who could comfort and protect me during scary times. Scary times like when Mom and Dad were arguing, and when I found myself alone at the party house. It is true that my experiences as a young girl contributed to my feeling of being alone. However, this aloneness haunted me. It was the kind of feeling that wouldn't go away in the presence of a crowd, in a circle of close friends, or even at Grandma's on a Sunday evening surrounded by family. It lingered, and at some point dug its claws deeply into my heart, along with its cousin—abandonment.

These nasty claws seemed to dig ever deeper as my life unfolded. Being one of the chubby girls in school, the teasing was ruthless. Why do people have to tell you things you already know in a rude and hurtful way? It really doesn't help. Whatever happened to, "If you don't have something nice to say, say nothing at all"? This golden rule of advice seems to have gone to the wayside of our world. Many times on the school playground, or during team sports in physical ed class, I would be picked last. Deeper the claws would go.

Challenges weren't left alone to the playground or P.E.—classrooms carried their own version. Math was my least favorite subject in school. Test days in math class were the absolute worst. I would wake up with a painful, nervous tummy that ached until my test was over. I can remember one test in particular in second or third grade where my nerves were shot and I didn't think I could even hold the pencil. It didn't help matters that we were having a very rare weather event that day. A thunderstorm decided to roll in, and like a spooky scene from a movie, the skies outside darkened. I literally thought I was going to die.

Growing up in California, rain was something we prayed for but never seemed to get enough of. My home state is one that cycles into a drought season often, and a thunderstorm was a very rare occurrence. In my entire first twenty-something years of life, we maybe had three thunderstorms that I can remember. As the test began, I decided to cross my fingers and my legs. Maybe, I thought, that would help me to stop shaking. My teacher began walking up and down the aisles to make sure no one was cheating. When she got to me, the rain outside started pounding louder on the building and my heart was pounding right along with it. My teacher stopped by my desk, looked at me, uncrossed my fingers, and said, "If you studied harder Kimberly, you wouldn't need luck!" It was like a death claw ripped a piece out of my heart. I longed for a black hole from space to just suck me away from it all.

Each school year came and went with its own share of drama and nerve-wracking moments. Being that I wasn't very popular, my friend groups were usually on the small side. One of my closest friends to this day is a girl that I have known since kindergarten. Now we are more like sisters than friends. In our younger years, life didn't offer enough opportunities for us to get together outside of school. However, we were much closer in high school, especially after I got a license and was able to pick her up and go hang out for the day. Our junior year was probably my favorite year of school. A new friend attended our school and we clicked immediately. A small group of us started hanging out more frequently, and it seemed I had a good friend group for the first time. We also started to attend our school's campus Christian Club. Two friendly students led the group, and they were so welcoming. Each week, I looked forward to Christian Club because it felt like family. It was a small place on campus where I actually felt I belonged. The leaders invited my friends and me to their youth group, and we decided to check it out. Soon, we were faithfully seeking Jesus with other kids weekly at youth group and it was breathing life into me. Between the campus club and youth group, it was like I became a part of something I was meant to belong to my entire life. I know it sounds cheesy, but hey, I was a teenager at the time!

Growing up, the feeling of belonging to a family was foreign to me. Mom and Dad both had their own challenges and work kept them both busy and exhausted. Although arguments were no longer common, Mom and Dad stuck to themselves. When they weren't working, Mom would spend time in the garden and Dad would spend time away from home playing golf with his friends. I spent most of my time alone, or with a few friends in the neighborhood. Mom was there for me to help with the occasional school project, or to do a puzzle on the weekend. I remember times where we would rearrange the living room furniture together, which always seemed to frustrate Dad. Mom and I would talk about anything and everything except for the past. We were indeed a family, but there was so much brokenness that I always felt alone, especially in my home.

The welcoming friends I began to meet at the youth group were like water to my soul. It was a place where I could come as I was, no strings attached, and just be. Youth leaders spoke such encouragement into my life and prayed with me. They were even praying for me throughout the week. When they asked how I was doing, it meant the world to me. This community of believers really cared about me, and it felt great. I really enjoyed going on ski retreats, especially my first one where I was able to see snow for the first time. I also loved it when we would get together with other youth groups in our area for youth conventions. It was like this huge family of people gathering together. It was the family of God. It was exactly where I belonged.

Looking back, I can see how the Miranda family was, in effect, God's family (God's love) reaching out to me. There was too much going on at the time for me to feel that family aspect of it. The pain of loneliness and feelings of abandonment seemed to blind me to the truth. The truth is, the moment I opened my heart and asked Jesus to be my Savior, I became a child of God. That famous verse from the Bible, John 3:16, tells us that God "so loved the world." His love compelled Him to send His son to die on behalf of our sins—on behalf of us. When we accept that gift of love and believe Jesus is our Savior, we immediately become part of God's family. We have a place where we belong and where we are beloved and not abandoned.

But to all who believed him and accepted him, he gave the right to become children of God. They are reborn – not with a physical birth resulting from human passion or plan, but a birth that comes from God. John 1:12–13

Truth doesn't change. I was indeed a child of God and thus part of His family. However, that deep, wounded place in my heart didn't yet believe it. The fullness of truth unfolds when it is married with our belief. Until then, it is more of a fact that seems distant from one's heart and soul. The Miranda family did a wonderful job of displaying love to me. The Christian Club and youth group were also avenues of God pouring out His love for me. I was pouring my heart out weekly to Jesus, and I became passionate about telling others that God loved them. Inside, though, I still battled feeling alone and abandoned. As I grew up, I came to realize that there is a difference in feeling loved by someone and knowing you are loved.

After graduating from high school, my life was full of community college classes, working as an administrative assistant for an insurance company, and volunteering as a youth leader. I was still living at home. Mom was working as a waitress, and Dad had entered retirement, which entailed spending even more time away from home golfing. I really enjoyed encouraging the youth group kids. Life can be very fulfilling when you are pouring into others. At one point, I reached out to the youth pastor and shared my desire to do more for God. He suggested I join the internship program— that I would be a "perfect fit." At the time, my desire to reach others and do whatever I could for Jesus overrode the wisdom of needing to pray about something before committing to it. That afternoon, I filled out an application and was accepted on the team. The next couple of months were crazy busy. Staff meetings and helping with the many responsibilities of being on the intern team took up a lot of my time. Grades were slipping, I was hardly home, tiredness was starting to set in on me. All of a sudden, what I once saw as a glamorous ministry opportunity was becoming an exhausting race for which I didn't quite feel fit.

One evening, it became evident that I just needed to pour my heart out to God. Why was I even doing this crazy internship if it was pulling at me left and right? Was it for Jesus? For the youth? To make my pastor happy? I've been a people pleaser for a long time, so maybe it was a bit of all of the above. Whatever it was, it was time for a real, honest look at my heart and this place in which I found myself. After thinking about it and allowing God to search my heart, He highlighted a few things. The first was the obvious fact that I jumped into this ministry with excitement instead of prayerful consideration and commitment. The second was that I felt the need to have a title, to belong in a deeper way and to have a purpose from a position. I had a picture in my mind of a few of the youth kids, the ones I poured into before the internship started. I saw them sitting alone and realized the busyness of this new commitment took me away from being free to pour into them. Yes, I was making an impact and pouring into the youth ministry through this new position. But I was forsaking a ministry in which God had already positioned me. It turns out God had used me in a powerful way without a title or position and now that was almost null and void due to the pull of ministry busyness. It wasn't the perfect fit for me after all, and I knew in my gut God was asking me to step down.

The deep feeling of loneliness that was embedded in my heart led me to crave recognition over authenticity. Loneliness and abandonment long for titles and positions as if it were an application of soul medication. In reality, it's just a bandage on a wound that needs a good cleaning and some spiritual stitches.

With a pounding heart, I found myself back in the youth pastor's office. The time came for a conversation I really didn't want to have. So my people-pleasing self had to be put on the shelf and an honest heart conversation needed to take place. After pouring out my confession, it was evident that this meeting wasn't going to go well. Mom actually joined me for the conversation—I was too scared to face it alone. What happened next was an utter shock to both of us. This pastor began to raise his voice at me and spoke in very condemning tones. Words became pressure that put the claws deeper into my heart. I was told I would never be successful at anything in life—not ministry, not college, not career, not marriage, not motherhood. If I couldn't keep a commitment, then I wasn't wanted anywhere near "his youth group." I was told to leave my key on his desk, collect my things from the intern office, and never set foot in "his church" again. My heart sank.

Soon after that, Mom stopped attending church. The hurt was too deep for her to ever go back there. That evening, I cried harder than I had ever cried before. This pastor was supposed to be a caring shepherd. While I probably deserved a reprimand, there was no compassion, no desire to help me look deeper at why I made the decision I did and no desire to help bring healing to my decision. The only thing on the table was my key and the only advice was to "go away." If this pastor was supposed to be a shepherd, he was not being a very good one. I felt like I was thrown to the wolves and branded a castaway.

Now, trust me for a minute in the telling of this truth. There are some very good shepherds in this world. Each of them fleshly humans who will make mistakes. If one of them has hurt you, it doesn't mean they will all hurt you. Jesus is the Good Shepherd, and I'll talk more about that later, as well as being hurt by the church. It's a nasty wound that needs to be addressed.

Just like Mom, I had a fleeting moment of thinking I, too, would never return to this specific church. However, somewhere along the way in life, Jesus blessed me with an immense gift of forgiveness. What I did know that evening was this: As hurt as I felt, there were still kids that God placed in my life to whom I could minister, and they were at that specific church. I heard the still, small yet powerful voice of Jesus speaking to my wounded heart: "My beloved, you go when I say to go. Right now, as hard as it may be for you, I need you to stay. These kids, into whom you are pouring, need you to stay in their lives for a little while longer. Trust me, dear one. I am with you."

With a broken heart, yet a renewed spirit to follow Jesus back into the very place of deep wounding, I was faithful to His call and continued attending church. I stepped down from a position in ministry, to minister to those Jesus had placed in my life organically. I continued pouring into the lives of youth and encouraging them to follow Jesus with all their hearts. I was able to resume writing encouraging notes to some of the youth again, able to take them to lunch or go for a walk at the park and just listen to what they were facing in life. I continued praying for the youth and shuttling whoever could fit into my car to and from the youth group. Some nights, I even made multiple trips in getting youth kids home. The difference Jesus made in my life as a young girl was so impactful. I didn't want anyone to miss out on that opportunity to learn about Jesus and His saving grace. The youth pastor never really spoke to me after that. An awkwardness sat between us. Basically I was there but not there in his eyes. People knew I wasn't an intern anymore, but no one really asked questions about why. That was the grace of God for me. I didn't talk about it out of respect for his position. He felt how he felt, and I knew God had me there for a purpose. So, in obedience, I stayed until God released me from that church.

Once I left, God led me to two small churches that shared the same building space. I found out about it through the Christian Fellowship Club at my community college. They had a huge college-age population at the Sunday night gathering, and I decided to give it a try. The worship was powerful, the people were on fire, and it seemed like a shelter and a sanctuary all wrapped in one—a safe place to land.

Around this time, worship became a huge draw for me. From my young girl days at VBS, I always enjoyed singing to Jesus. Worshiping God started to become a salve for my hurting heart in many ways. My heart's desire to worship led me to learn guitar. One afternoon, Dad came with me to the local music store, and I purchased my first acoustic guitar. We found out about a guy who would come to your house for lessons and I signed up. Thursday afternoons became one of my favorite times of the week. The worst part was building up my callouses. Who knew pushing little strings down could hurt so bad? Eventually, I learned chords and was able to play a few worship songs here and there. I would spend hours in worship, alone in my room. For the first time in a long time, although I was alone, the feeling of loneliness and abandonment began to fade.

Two years passed and I was now working full-time for the insurance company and still living with Mom and Dad. A good friend of mine from the old church asked if I would join her for a college/career-aged fellowship group. Basically, it was a life group for young adults. I figured it couldn't hurt, and I wouldn't have to run into the youth pastor because the life group was held at someone's apartment. During this time of my life, I decided to do a silly challenge and see how long it would take for me to see one license plate from every state in the country. So, I kept my eye out for out-of-state plates and checked them off my list. When we pulled into the apartment parking lot, I noticed a car with a Virginia license plate. A smile crossed my face. It's the little things sometimes that can make you smile. Another state checked off the list. I placed a satisfied checkmark on the paper next to Virginia. Silly as it may be, it put a skip in my step. I was looking forward to a night with a good friend and a chance to make some new friends as well. That very night, I met my husband, John, from Virginia!

Needless to stay, I kept attending the life group and it ushered in fresh life. Now, this chapter isn't about how we met and fell in love. I do know, though, that God brought a sweet, southern boy all the way to California just for me. Many friendships developed in the coming months. John played guitar and ended up leading worship for the life group. We started to get to know each other more and when he found out I played guitar, he asked me to join him as he led each week. I didn't know all the chords he did, and he encouraged me to play what I knew and skip the rest. We ended up walking to our cars together at the end of life group each week. Our conversations seemed to get longer and longer under the starry sky. It was a really sweet time.

Eventually, we started dating. We would go for picnics, drives up the Northern California coast, and hikes, all the while getting to know each other more and more. More evenings than not, I found myself getting off of work, stopping by the grocery store, then heading to John's apartment to cook dinner. We would eat, clean up, and play board games, or put a puzzle together while we listened to worship music. After about a year of dating, John asked Dad for my hand in marriage. He proposed on top of Mount Diablo, a mountain in our county where we spent a lot of time hiking. I said, "YES!" After four months of engagement, we married near my hometown on August 10, 2002. It was a beautiful day. I felt so loved and cherished. For the first time, I thought my heart would burst from happiness. There were a lot of favorite moments from our special day. One of them was the unity candle—two flames uniting into one; two lives becoming one. It was a powerful display of the promise we were making to each other and to God. My other favorite moment was when we got in the car to drive away and it was just the two of us. The beginning of a beautiful adventure.

Had I let bitterness keep me from returning to a church that wounded me, I would have never met John. Thankfully, God hadn't allowed my heart to harden that way. Allowing forgiveness to flow from my heart paved the way for a blessing of which I could have never dreamed. Our honeymoon consisted of driving a U-Haul truck across the country with my Toyota 4-Runner being towed behind us. It wasn't a dream honeymoon, but I felt like I was living a dream. John accepted a software engineering job in Atlanta, Georgia, and had lived there since January. After our wedding night, we finished loading up the U-Haul with family and then we headed out across the country, just the two of us, from California to Georgia. It was an adventurous start to our marriage journey.

As a little girl, I remember wanting nothing more than to someday be a wife and mother. That chapter of my life was just beginning, yet I felt ill-prepared for it. John has been such a loving and kind husband from the very beginning. He is a southern gentleman, loves Jesus, and he is the perfect match for me. I was so excited to start this new chapter of life with him and looked forward to living in a new state for the first time in my life. Actually, it was my first move ever. I lived in the same house from the day Mom and Dad brought me home from the hospital until the night before my wedding. When we crossed the California/Arizona border, it was indeed bittersweet. The rearview mirror of life is a small window into the past. Everything that has happened in it brings us to where we are this very moment. Those past moments have shaped us and formed who we are. The good and the bad have brought us to the present. The windshield of life, however, holds vast opportunities. I believe where we are going is more important than where we have been. When driving a vehicle, it would be to our own detriment if we were to only look in the rearview mirror. Eventually, we would crash. However, that rearview mirror is there for a reason and it cannot be ignored. There are times when life is cruising along in the fast lane—those things we once thought were behind us can catch up to us. It's good to see them coming and take time to deal with them. But sometimes those things of the past catch us off guard. It's then that, in this race called life, we are forced to make a pit stop.

Five long days of driving brought us to Atlanta during traffic hour. Eventually, we made it safely to our apartment. We were home. The home where we would begin our lives together. That night we unloaded the U-Haul with a friend John met at church. The next morning, we enjoyed breakfast and sat down to open our wedding gifts and make a list for thank-you cards. After returning the U-Haul, it was time to hit the road again. We headed up to Virginia for a wedding celebration with John's side of the family. Celebrations in John's family, called "hootenannies," consisted of food, fun, and sing-alongs. Uncles, cousins, and family friends would bring their guitars and sing hymns, old country songs, and southern rock. I guess I didn't know just how southern my husband was. We enjoyed celebrating with family and friends alike. My family enlarged the day I got married, and the loving, welcoming spirit they extended was beautiful.

That first year of marriage was hard. While I knew that John loved me and I felt very secure in his love, those feelings of loneliness and abandonment began to catch up with me. We decided to trust God for our family planning, and it turned out after one monthly cycle, the next one never came. I was pregnant. We were in love, happy, and nervous all at the same time. We were in our early twenties and it was our desire to have children while we were young, so we would have the energy to chase after them! Little did we know how fast that would come to fruition. Hormones were flooding my body, and I began really missing family and friends in California. When we were engaged, I desperately missed John, as he was already living in Georgia. Now that we were married, I had the love of my life, but everyone I ever knew was 2,481 very long miles away. It was such a hard adjustment for me. I was thankful for a loving husband who wasn't afraid of my tears and would hold me close as I wept.

In that first year of marriage, we moved from our apartment into our first home, had our first child, and celebrated our first anniversary. Though it was a hard transition, it was a great first year of marriage. Being that we had no family around us, it was a year of forging our marriage, which drew us closer to each other. Looking back, I wouldn't have wanted it to be any different. The foundation of our marriage was Jesus, and that first year really allowed us to build strongly on what we would need to carry us through. The two of us had truly become one and we were on our way to having a loving family of our own. Our journey of marriage mingled with parenthood, and we were living life to the full.

The church we were attending was very welcoming, and we started to develop wonderful friendships. The southern hospitality that many families showed us by bringing meals and inviting us over for a game night and dinner turned out to be just what we needed. God was extending His love to us through the family of God and it was a beautiful thing. The ladies at church threw me a baby shower and lavished us with meals for weeks after our daughter was born. I never realized how powerful a home-cooked meal, brought in love, could be. Through this extension of love, God started changing my heart about those feelings of loneliness and abandonment.

All of those feelings came to a head one year as Christmas was approaching. It would be the first year that we weren't able to travel to be with family for Christmas. On the way home from shopping, with my young daughter in the back seat, tears started to flow. I was praying and telling God how it was so hard for me to be away from family during the holidays. The holidays were all about being with family after all, right? Yes, it was true that the body of Christ was becoming my family when I found myself living miles away from all I had ever known. However, the long months of being separated from loved ones was coming to a head in my heart.

I could hear God's still small voice say, "Beloved, Christmas is indeed about family. It's about my family, being torn apart so that my Son could come and make a way for you to be part of my family forever. All these moments that you feel you are missing out with loved ones, I redeem them. I am a relational God and restoration is one of my best works. Each moment of loneliness and abandonment you feel, my Son felt first on your behalf. In my great love for you, I gave my one and only Son, extending salvation and adoption to all mankind. You are never alone, and my love is always with you. Let me take these claws from your heart and plant my seeds of love. Trust in my plans for you and know that I indeed make all things beautiful in their time. Every moment you and your family experience in eternity with me will redeem the lonely moments you experience on earth. I am making all things new. You are my beloved daughter and I am with you always—you are never alone."

Healing tears began flowing in overdrive and I had to pull to the side of the road. I can't explain how He speaks to me, but when He does, I know His voice well.

He sent out his word and healed them, snatching them from the door of death. Psalm 107:20

Loneliness and abandonment were trying to steal life from my heart and soul. It wasn't physical death, but an emotional death from which His words saved me. His Word, the Bible began to come alive to me as I dove into it more and more. I was reminded that Jesus called Himself the "Word made flesh." Jesus, the Word of God, was sent out from His own family in heaven to heal me. God's love was being revealed to me in healing ways, and it was transforming my heart.

One of the best gifts that God gives us is the gift of His presence. I am sure that in the moments and days after Christ's ascension, His followers felt very alone. However, Jesus said it was good for Him to go away so His Spirit could come and fill His followers.

But in fact, it is best for you that I go away, because if I don't, the Advocate won't come. If I do go away, then I will send him to you. John 16:7

The Advocate here is the Holy Spirit, who is our Comforter and Counselor—the Spirit of God living in a believer. The Holy Spirit seals our position in God's family. We are safe and secure in His kingdom. He will never leave us. We fit into the family of God. His love draws us into His forever family, and we belong there. Beloved, you fit right into the center of God's great love. He never abandons us, no matter what your past or present circumstances tell you—no matter what the future throws at you. When we stand on these truths of God's Word, they are a solid foundation. Allow His words to flood healing into the deepest places of your heart. You are His beloved. So be loved and know that you are never, never alone. *Do not be afraid, for I have ransomed you. I have called you by name; you are mine. When you go through deep waters, I will be with you. When you go through rivers of difficulty, you will not drown. When you walk through the fire of oppression, you will not be burned up; the flames will not consume you. Isaiah 43:1–2*

As His love was lavished on me and revealed through so many ways, I began to truly believe I was loved. It's who I am, and walking in that identity has made all the difference. The Bible tells us that when Jesus walked this earth He created, He often withdrew to lonely places. In those places, He would pray to the Father. His love compelled Him to come, and the joy set before Him enabled Him to endure the cross. That joy, I believe, was us. He knew that on the other side of the cross, there was an empty grave. That the work of Calvary, the pouring out of His blood, indeed of His love, well, it would cancel the curse of sin and allow His love to draw us into the family of God. He cried out on that cross, in a moment of abandonment like no other will ever face. He faced it on our behalf. It is never His intention for us to feel that abandonment. We are meant to feel His overwhelming and never-ending love forever.

May His great love for you and the truth that you are His joy and delight encourage you to endure anything that comes your way. You are His beloved and you forever belong in the center of His love.

Chapter 3

HOPE-GOOD FATHER

F ather of lies versus the Good Father—it's an epic battle. It's a boxing match for the heart of mankind fought in the ring within each of us. In one corner, the Good Father stands firm and strong with a title He will always defend. In the other corner, an imposter and enemy to us all, the father of lies with his feeble attempt to sucker punch our Good Father. For a long time, it felt like I was in the middle of the ring, taking all the punches. The Good Father, who I knew from a young age, was truly in my corner and had my back, seemed to somehow allow me to be in the middle of the ring. The father of lies, pummeling me with every chance he could get, doesn't come close to the Good Father.

During the early years, when Mom was fighting her demons, I remember climbing into bed with Dad at night. At the time, I had no clue he was fighting his own demons from the bottle. He was the safe place to run to in the dark of night when Mom wasn't around. I would fall asleep to the sound of Dad reciting his Hail Marys (the sole extent of his Catholic faith). One night, I decided to chew some gum, thinking that would help calm my nervous tummy. As I slept, the gum slipped out of my mouth, landing in my Dad's thick, black hair. Dad fumed the next morning and flames of fear licked at me. Dad yelled at me and as his temper rose out, it had a way of tempering me—had its way of pushing me away.

Coloring was a form of creativity and escape for me from early on in life. It was a huge stress reliever as well. I would often pull out a piece of blank paper and a pile of crayons and get lost in the colors and imagination. Dad was in his room, sitting at his desk looking serious. Mom wasn't around. Timidly, I interrupted Dad to ask for some paper and crayons, only to be ignored. Determined to color, I recalled a tube of lipstick Mom left in the hall bathroom cabinet. While it wasn't a crayon, it would do just fine. I snuck into my room with the flower wallpaper and sat in the corner. As life was swirling around me, I began to draw a swirl design on the wall—bigger and bigger it got. I was just at the point where I had to stand up to make my swirl even bigger, when around the corner Dad came. His eyes were so very big, and the fuming temper raged in his raised voice. A few minutes later, his strong hand that was supposed to protect me was smacking my behind. It was one of the few times I received such punishment, but it was enough to make me plan an escape.

After a lot of shed tears in my room alone, it was time to leave. I had enough and packed up a few things in a pillowcase and grabbed my treasured dolly. The pain of everything built up to this moment. If Dad's hand was going to hurt instead of protect, if he couldn't help make Mom better and keep me safe from her struggles, if, if, if. Well, if this is how it was going to be, I was out. So out of my room I ran, and into the hallway I went, only to turn around and go straight back to my room. What was I thinking? Where in the world would a young girl like me go? I knew the street where I lived and how to get to a few places in town. I had always been very observant, so that would help. However, reality struck me. As afraid as I was of the chaos at home, I was more terrified of the possibility of what could lie beyond the front door. The world was just too scary to navigate alone with dolly and Jesus, so I unpacked my pillowcase and decided to tough it out at home. I would be quiet and reserved and stick to myself, careful to not create any unwanted waves.

Dad's temper could fume, but it didn't happen often. That was something for which to be thankful. There were actually many fond memories I had with Dad growing up. One of my most treasured memories was picking out a Christmas tree each year. As the end of November would roll around and the tree lots started going up, I felt the excitement building. It was a highlight of the year to pick out the tree with Dad. Mom returned home and our dysfunctional family was functioning the best it knew how. Mom would stay home and get out the tree stand and ornaments while Dad and I went on our tree-selecting adventure. To this day, the smell of pine brings me back to those early years as I ran through the lot looking for the perfect tree. Dad and I would even play hide-and-seek a bit, as we eyed the trees on the lot. With the selection made and the tree secured to the top of the car, we were off. Getting the tree from the car and into the house was always a wrestling match. Dad was never one to have the gift of patience. The joyous adventure of selecting the perfect tree was always dampened by his frustrations at setting it up. The enemy of my soul would whisper, "Joy never lasts. Good will always be mixed with bad."

On multiple occasions, Dad promised to take me somewhere like the park, bowling, or minigolf. His promises to finally put Christmas lights on the house and to play checkers with me were just empty words. As much as Dad enjoyed golf, there was one thing he didn't seem to understand. Just as your stroke in golf is only good if you follow through, your promises are the same. Otherwise, those promises are just empty words. In time, the mention of a promise began to cause pain to my heart. I couldn't begin to realize and trust the promise when the follow-through never came.

This lack of follow-through on my dad's part shaped the way I viewed God. As a believer, it was hard for me to see God as a father, let alone a good one. The father of lies worked overtime throwing reminder punches my way, trying so very hard to blind me from seeing God as a Good Father.

As you know, life eventually found me living in Georgia. John and I were happily married and navigating the journey of raising a family of our own. Those sucker-punch lies from the enemy followed me. Early in marriage, I would have dreams that John left me. In the dreams, he would leave a note or a nasty voicemail saying he never wanted to see me again. I'd try calling his parents to see if they could talk some sense into him and they didn't answer. I would be left alone with the baby and a small couch and the dream would fade. These were the kind of dreams that felt so real, I would wake up crying. John never gave me a reason to doubt his love, and we determined that divorce would never come for us. But John's love was a promise to me, and I didn't have a good history with promises. Those lies of the enemy became another hook that tormented my dreams. They didn't happen all the time, but it was this way of the enemy trying to have me doubt my husband's love for me. When you aren't secure in the knowledge of the Good Father's love, that insecurity can flow into any other relationship.

Although saddened by the fact that I would even have those kinds of dreams, John was always there for me. He would hug me and reassure me of his love and his promise to never leave me. We were committed to each other for life, and he would remind me that I was the perfect wife for him—remind me that I was God's gift to him. Those reminders of the truth enabled me to discount the lies the enemy was trying to speak. When we were married, I decided to continue wearing my engagement ring closest to my heart and have my wedding ring on the outside of it, closer to my knuckle. It was a way that I could daily remind myself that John first promised to marry me, then sealed that promise by marrying me. His promise of love became a healing treasure for me, as it still is to this day.

John's loving nature as a father also became a healing treasure for me. He was patient and willing to spend quality time with our daughter. He demonstrated how much he valued her by taking her on father-daughter dates, and dancing with her in the living room. He was gentle and kind. Most importantly he followed through on his promises. Eventually, our family grew with the birth of our son. You never know how much more your heart can love until your family grows. Those precious newborn moments with our oldest daughter holding her baby brother are so very special. As our adventures in parenthood continued, I was very careful when it came to promising my children anything. In fact, other than promising before God to love John as my husband for life, I wasn't big on making promises. I never wanted to leave a wound of an unfollowed promise on the hearts of my children. I was determined to only promise something if I knew for sure I could follow through. There were times when my children would ask me to promise them I would play a game with them later in the day. My response would always be, "Yes, to the best of my ability, we will play a game later today." I would tell them that promises are special and not to be made lightly. Often, I would tell them that the one truth I could promise them in this life is that God would love them forever and I would do my best to love them all the days of their lives. I wanted to make sure I protected them from broken promises.

When promises are broken, anger can settle in. I struggled in those early years of parenthood. Not that I am a perfect parent now, but I have come a long way. Early on, I would be angry a lot. The exhaustion of parenthood, the demand, the way the kids needed me *so much*, all seemed too much. While the demons my parents faced with the bottle never came after me, it seemed anger hooked me through broken promises of the past. I remember feeling like my kids were leeches and I longed for some time to myself. I was really good at keeping quiet and out of the way as a child. Why couldn't they? When a child grows up in a healthy home, they naturally test their parents, seeing where the safe boundaries are. Our kids were great with other people, but they sure seemed to test me a lot. I loved my children dearly, but goodness, Momma needs a timeout here and there. The fuming frustrations that once made my dad raise his voice at me became the go-to behavior for me at times. I hated it when I would raise my voice in frustration at my children. Those strong feelings of anger seemed to just flow so easily, and I didn't understand why. My husband was so loving, my kids were healthy, and we had a beautiful home to call our own. We were figuring out how to be good stewards of our finances so our bills were paid, we had food on the table, and we had a good circle of friends.

I remember once being so frustrated and angry at myself for raising my voice at my daughter. While talking with John about it one night, I just started to cry and ran to the garage to sit in my car. I felt like that scared little girl all over again. Hiding in the car made me feel safe. John came after me and just held me as the tears flowed. The protective walls that I built started to melt away. The love of my husband at that moment was like the love of Christ for the church—his bride! It came to rescue me and soothe the pain in my heart. I began to realize that I needed Jesus to heal those old wounds from my earthly father. I needed to learn how to trust God as a Good Father.

None of that happened overnight. But that rescuing embrace started me on a journey to seek God as a Good Father. I will never know the reasons why my dad made promises he couldn't keep. We all do that to some degree. As a young girl, it felt like a wounding to my value as a person. The father of lies would speak in those moments, "If he valued you at all, he would follow through for you." We each love others in our lives the best way we know how. We love in our own broken way. It's never going to be perfect, but that didn't mean my dad's broken version of love wasn't love. He was just loving me the best he could. The same went for Mom. I'll never understand life from my dad's shoes, or what wounds he faced that shaped him into who he is. That's not really for me to figure out.

What I did need to figure out was how to defeat the lies so I could see God as a Good Father.

One of the ways that God started to reveal Himself to me as a Good Father was through our move from Georgia to New Jersey. At the end of 2008, the stock market was crashing, the housing market bubble was bursting, and God was moving our family from Georgia to New Jersey. My husband was offered a software engineering job in New York City! We faced this job offer as we did job offers of the past. From the start of our relationship, we came to God in prayer over major decisions. Early on, before we were engaged, John was offered two software jobs. One was in Atlanta and one was in Seattle. It had been a dream of mine to live in the Pacific Northwest ever since a road trip my dad and I took in my late teen years. I love rain, mountains, evergreen trees, and fresh air, and the Pacific Northwest had it all. When John was faced with these two different job offers, we decided to pray and ask God what He had for us. We knew we wanted to get married eventually and we wanted to make this decision together. So after a few days of seeking God's will through prayer, we shared our hearts with each other. Both of us felt that John was supposed to take the job in Atlanta, and that is indeed what he did. So we followed God's leading in obedience and I shelved the dream of living in the Pacific Northwest. At the time, I was crushed but God would teach me a valuable lesson through this. About a year after we were married, the company in Seattle went out of business. Had we not taken the time to prayerfully consider where God was leading, we would have found ourselves with a new baby and without a job. Obedience can protect us from many things!

After praying over this New York job offer, we felt God leading us to take it. Our hearts' desire as a married couple was to hear God's voice above all the others and to follow Him in obedience. Originally, we were going to wait to move to New Jersey until the end of the school year. Our oldest daughter was halfway into her kindergarten year and we didn't really want to pull her out mid-year. The company in New York City was going to allow John to work from home until school got out in June. However, once a month, he would have to travel to NYC for a week to work in their office. We didn't want to be separated for a week each month and decided on moving in the middle of December. Trusting God would provide for us, we put our house up for sale.

I remember asking God for favor with moving companies because we needed flexibility when it came to details. We were working with a realtor to find a home to rent in New Jersey, but we didn't have an area pinned down just yet. I called three companies to obtain moving quotes and all three of them told me they were very flexible. I was so thankful God was opening doors for us. It turns out that, at the time, I wasn't really thinking clearly in regard to all that was going on with the housing markets, et cetera. As the financial world was trying not to collapse, many people were moving out of the Northeast, especially out of NYC with lost jobs. God used this bad situation for our good and provided a home to rent and the flexibility with the moving company that we needed. A Good Father provides for His children. And slowly those sucker-punch lies in the ring of life started to not land as hard. In fact, I think I was learning to dodge a few of them.

Not only did God provide for our move up to New Jersey, but he provided a buyer for our Georgia home in about four months. This new job allowed us the provision to cover a mortgage in Georgia and rent in New Jersey for that time, which in itself was a miracle. It was also a housing-market miracle that our house was able to sell in such a short time in the midst of a huge economic crisis. We were very thankful for all of God's provision and for this new chapter of life.

Now moving to the Northeast in the middle of winter from Georgia had challenges of its own. This California girl had to learn to drive in the snow, which was scary at first. John had to figure out how to get in and out of the biggest city in the country, and sometimes his commute was affected when the president of the United States happened to fly into the city for an event. The biggest challenge came during our first week in New Jersey, when my dad had a massive stroke. With my husband starting his new job the very next day, and my daughter needing to be registered for school, I found myself stuck on the East Coast. I didn't know if my dad would survive, or what condition he would be in. All I could do was pray and wait for the phone calls from Mom for an update. Thankfully Dad survived the stroke; however, his life drastically changed overnight. With some muscle weakness on the left side of his body, he would never play golf or bowl again.

Living close to NYC, we experienced the crossroads of the world. It was a very exciting time in our lives. We were settling in, and one of our favorite things about this chapter of our lives was our church. New friendships were forming. There was a life group that allowed us to bring our young children along. The worship was wonderful and the pastors a delight. God provided another part of His great big family for us to join and we couldn't have been more blessed by it. One of the phrases that caught fire in my heart was something the lead pastor would often say, "You are safe and secure in the kingdom of God." This phrase became life to my bones every time I heard it. It was like God the Father speaking through my new pastor, directly to my wounded heart. At the same time, faith was rising up in my spirit to actually believe the words to be true.

One of the huge blessings out of this season came in the form of company trips. We were able to travel to Cancun and Cabo, Mexico, and experience wonderful, dream-like beach vacations. Being that we lived so far apart, our vacations were usually spent traveling to see and spend time with family. Life didn't afford us time for any other type of vacation, let alone the funds for one. Those trips were like God the Father lavishing us with His goodness. It was more than we could think or imagine on our own, and we were so very thankful for these wonderful blessings. Those vacations were a gift we didn't know we needed, let alone something we would have thought to ask God for.

So if you sinful people know how to give good gifts to your children, how much more will your heavenly Father give good gifts to those who ask him. Matthew 7:11

A hard, painful, and scary childhood shaped the way I viewed the world in many ways. Yet it was also true that my parents, as imperfect people, loved me the best they knew how. Mom and Dad both worked very hard to provide for me. They chose to stay together under the same roof so that I didn't have to be passed between them. They honestly spoiled me rotten, except I never really acted rotten. We did share times of laughter, joy, and moments I will always treasure. I witnessed a softening to my dad as I got older. The look in his eyes as he prepared to give me away on my wedding day was a look of deep affection I hadn't seen before. And when I had children of my own, my dad turned into a papa that melted with love for his grandchildren.

My parents had their faults, but it didn't mean they were completely bad. They were capable of much good, and I am thankful for each of the many ways they showed goodness to me. As hard as it was, it could have been worse. However, the negative things that were deposited in me as a child became the left hooks I had to deal with later in life. But God, the Good Father, was revealing Himself to me and helping me see through His eyes. It is vital that we see man through God's eyes instead of seeing God through the actions of man. It makes all the difference!

In John 14:9, Jesus tells one of His disciples, Philip, *"Anyone who has seen me has seen the Father!"* Reading that brought it all together for me. From a very young age, I sang songs of Jesus's love for me. I read stories of how Jesus came to live a life that poured into others.

He healed the sick, spoke words of encouragement and life into so many. Forgiving sins, Jesus went to the cross and rose again. Jesus, love incarnate, walked this earth on our behalf. He revealed the heart of His Father to mankind. What we read about Jesus is therefore true of the Father. Jesus valued us so much that he was willing to die for us. A Good Father is willing to lay down His own life for His children. Growing up, I had no problem believing Jesus loved me. Now grown, I was realizing Jesus's love reflected the Father perfectly, and the Father was indeed good.

What is the price of two sparrows – one copper coin? But not a single sparrow can fall to the ground without your Father knowing it. And the very hairs on your head are all numbered. So don't be afraid; you are more valuable to God than a whole flock of sparrows.
Matthew 10:29–31

Beloved, the Good Father highly values you. He put it all on the line for you. Never doubt that truth. No matter how the enemy sucker punches you with lies, I pray the love of the Good Father will be your shield. I pray that as you walk in the knowledge that you are loved dearly by a Good Father, it will help you to dodge every punch the enemy throws your way. I pray that you will know the Good Father is indeed in your corner, cheering you on, speaking good things over you, and that He doesn't miss a moment of your life. He longs to turn the bad into good and bless you beyond measure. May your eyes be opened to seeing the truth of the Goodness of your Abba Father, your Daddy God. And may every lie-punch the enemy has landed be healed by the Good Father's great love for you. Remember that the enemy is really only throwing sucker punches. On Calvary, Jesus reflecting the perfect love of the Good Father landed the ultimate knockout punch to the father of lies. With the Good Father in your corner and the truth of His love in your heart, you will be victorious against every lie of the enemy.

A quick word of encouragement for those of us who have been the one helping land punches for the father of lies. For those of us who have thrown our own punches of pain at others. Remember that this Good Father has been looking for you to turn and come home. His heart for the prodigal beats strongly.

So he returned home to his father. And while he was still a long way off, his father saw him coming. Filled with love and compassion, he ran to his son, embraced him and kissed him. Luke 15:20

No matter how far we are from the Father, He sees us right where we are. He longs for us to come running into His great arms of love. He has a robe, sandals, and a ring waiting for us. He longs to call us His own. If you are feeling far from the Father, or have never felt close to Him, just turn around. He's been waiting there all along and He is Good!

Chapter 4

HOPE-PEACE

Fear is the opposite of peace. At least that is what I have experienced on a number of occasions in life. For a long time, my nature was to be fearful and worry over just about everything. When John and I got married, it took me a while to feel at peace during a southern thunderstorm. Those few storms I experienced as a child in California were no match for the good ol' thunder whompers of the South! Since John grew up with these intense storms, he was able to sleep right through them. All the while I would lay awake wondering if a tornado would touch down and suck us up to a land over the rainbow. To put it simply, I was a chicken, y'all.

A few months after moving to Georgia, we had one such thunder whomper roll through in the middle of the night. It always has to be the middle of the night with these monsters, doesn't it? The sound of rain was something I enjoyed, and it would put me to sleep faster than anything in the world. On this particular night, I remember the sense of lights flashing eventually waking me up. My first thought was that there was a police car outside in the apartment complex parking lot. "That must be what is flashing light so brightly," I thought. I got up to peek out the window and, in the distance, I could see the sky lighting up. It was like some little kid in heaven was turning the lights on and off. No actual lightning strikes were visible, but as the approaching storm closed in, they began to come into view. Thunder started rumbling and only grew louder as the storm drew close.

I didn't have a good feeling about this storm. Okay, to be honest, I didn't have a good feeling about any of them. Full panic mode was setting in on me, and being a good wife, I thought it best to wake my husband so we could be there for each other if this was the storm that would take us out! We decided to check out the weather report on TV and take a look at the radar just in case. There was a severe thunderstorm headed our way. While the weathermen of the country do the best they can, they don't always know exactly when or where a tornado will form. John was a dear and reminded me that Georgia didn't really experience tornados like other parts of the country. My mom grew up in Missouri, and I heard her stories of green-tinted skies, unplugging electronics, and taking shelter in the hall closet. In fact, she gave me tips on what to do if a tornado ever came my way. My fears were telling me this was that kind of storm. My husband sat on the couch watching the weather updates and decided to open the sliding glass door a bit in case the telltale train sound began. The town warning sirens were going off, due to the severe thunderstorm warning. Meanwhile, I went into the bedroom and got fully dressed. Grabbing a flashlight and a battery-operated radio, I put them in the bathroom. Then I ran into the living room to get John and tried to convince him to pull the mattress off our bed as a protective cover and hide in the bathtub with me. If this storm was going to throw down a tornado, I wanted to be ready.

When I arrived in the living room, we both heard that train-like sound. This was it. We were going to die right there in our apartment if I didn't die of a heart attack first. I ran to John. The look of concern on his face brought no comfort. Then it hit—not a tornado, but the truth of our circumstance finally hit us. It was at that moment we both realized a fact we overlooked in the midst of our storm. Our apartment was located pretty close to a set of train tracks that went through our town. As we took a closer listen, we could hear an actual train rolling by. We shared mutual sighs of relief. John kind of gave me a funny look, realizing that I had gotten fully dressed. I guess it was silly, but what did I know? This was my first thunder whomper and fear got the best of me. Eventually, the storm passed, and we were able to fall back asleep, securely planted on the earth, far from the land over the rainbow.

In all honesty, I didn't have much peace in the middle of that storm. Like most situations that caused fear, my peace seemed to only come after the calming of the storm. Was peace in the middle of the storm even possible? I often heard testimonies of people saying God brought them peace in the storm, but up to this point, it wasn't something I ever experienced as the norm in the storm. How my heart longed for that steadying peace.

Jesus and his disciples experienced a storm of their own. In the books of Matthew, Mark, and Luke, Jesus's disciples tell their testimony of a scary moment on the water. At this point in their literal walk with Jesus, these faithful followers saw many amazing things. Jesus called each of them by name. In and of itself, this was a high honor. They had been on hand to see the formation of the original twelve disciples. They witnessed Jesus teaching the masses through His famous sermon on the mount. Luke tells us in the seventh chapter of his book that Jesus brought a young boy back to life—resurrection power displayed before their very eyes. These first followers of Jesus saw him cast out demons from those who were being tormented. Jesus also healed many people as they journeyed from town to town with Him. In fact, the night they crossed the lake, Jesus touched many people in the town of Capernaum.

That evening many demon-possessed people were brought to Jesus. He cast out the evil spirits with a simple command, and he healed all the sick. Matthew 8:16

43

Did you see the last part of that verse? It was just another day in the life of Jesus, casting out evil spirits and healing *all* the sick. *All.* While we aren't given a number, we know that all who were sick that came to Jesus that night received a healing touch. On the heels of this mass healing, the disciples followed Jesus into a boat and proceeded in crossing the lake. At some point, smooth sailing went to the wayside.

Suddenly, a fierce storm struck the lake, with waves breaking into the boat. But Jesus was sleeping. The disciples went and woke him up, shouting, "Lord, save us! We're going to drown!" Matthew 8:24–25

I have heard it said that "Jesus changes everything." What happens to His followers when suddenly everything changes? How do we react when these suddenlies of life hit? Fear was a go-to for me. My husband has had a very strong measure of faith since he was little. He is also a pretty peaceful guy. That faith of His gave Him a steadying peace. I trusted Jesus to be my Lord, but my faith was not very strong when the sudden moments hit. I often left the faith to John and chose to huddle in my worry corner, fearful of the many "what ifs," that scream to us in the storms of life. Like those disciples, I was afraid in the boat. I faced each storm in life with a suspicion that it could, in fact, be the one to take me out. In the middle of any given storm, my reaction would be similar to that of these first followers of Christ. "Jesus, am I going to drown?"

Just like the disciples, you can walk with Jesus for some time and still struggle with having peace in the middle of the storms. And just like the disciples, the storms can teach us valuable lessons that amaze us. That first year of marriage brought me to a place where I learned one such lesson. It was a moment where the peace I needed flooded over me at just the right time.

Life was sailing along smoothly. John and I moved from our little apartment in Georgia into our first home. We were settling in and getting the nursery ready for our first child. My pregnancy was progressing well with no hiccups or challenges in sight. Other than a bit of nervousness about actually pushing the baby out, I was very much looking forward to birth and holding our baby for the first time. My due date had come and gone. The doctor said, "It could be any day now!" The following week, during a routine checkup, the doctor informed me that my baby was floating. At first, I thought that was normal. After all, the baby was surrounded by water, hadn't the baby been floating all along? Yes, the baby was floating around in water, but the week prior her head was down and engaged and ready for delivery. Now, she seemed to be floating backward away from the birth canal. The doctor said that sometimes this is the baby's way of signaling that it will not fit through the birth canal. The possibility of a C-section was now a reality. Being that I was now overdue, I was sent for an ultrasound to check the baby's weight. It was then decided that I be admitted to the labor and delivery department at the hospital and given something to soften my cervix to help aid in bringing on labor. So, for the first time in my life, I was admitted to a hospital.

Our desired birth plan was for everything to be as natural as possible. At this point, it looked like I was going to need a kick-start. The first attempt to get my body a little help with going into labor didn't work. I was able to take a shower and then they told me they would start the dreaded Pitocin to induce labor. Pitocin is a synthetic version of the body's natural hormone oxytocin, which helps your uterus contract during labor. Pitocin, however, brings your body into labor at a much harsher rate than the natural stuff. My body may not have naturally known to go into labor, but the Pitocin definitely started working and soon I was in the throes of it. The intensity of the Pitocin then made me throw my natural birth plan out the window. First, I had some meds to help with pain— then I was crying for the epidural. Soon enough, it was time to push. However, after doing that for about an hour, the baby wasn't progressing and seemed to be stuck. The doctor decided to back off on the epidural pain medication to see if that would help me feel the urge to push. All I felt was intense pain, and the doctor decided I needed a C-section to get the baby out safely. Fear flooded my body. Honestly, a C-section was my worst birthing fear and it was suddenly upon me.

The medical staff rushed me into the operating room and my husband waited outside while they prepared me for surgery. Unfortunately, because they backed off on my epidural, they needed to get that going again so I would be numb for the procedure. The fifteen-minute prep time turned into forty-five minutes. The anesthesiologist had a look of concern, then made a call to the doctor. I had areas where I was completely numb, but I was still feeling the pinprick test in a variety of places. The medical team was talking in the background about possibly having to put me to sleep if the next epidural dose of medication didn't work. I was so scared. The last thing I wanted was to be asleep during the birth of my baby. None of this was turning out as I expected. I looked up at the ceiling tile and my heart cried, "Jesus." Suddenly, I was reminded of the many family and friends that were praying for me at that moment. The peace of Jesus flooded my entire body. The epidural finally started working, and the next thing I knew they were bringing John into the room. A little after midnight, while I was flooded with peace, our sweet baby girl came into the world. She was healthy, and we couldn't have been happier.

I have to say that this was the first time I felt such a tremendous amount of God's peace in the middle of a sudden moment of life. While the situation didn't end up turning out how I would have hoped, I would not trade experiencing that peace for anything in the world. We can hear stories about others having peace, but until we experience it for ourselves, we don't really know how powerful it is. It was the same for the disciples. Although they saw the power of God on display through His son, Jesus, they needed to also experience His power for themselves. When we follow Jesus, we can be sure that there will be storms along the way. He will lead us into boats and onto lakes where "suddenly" moments will happen. These are the moments that can usher in His peace that passes all understanding. They are moments that can build our faith and trust in Him. Moments where His word-promises to us can come alive.

I have told you all this so that you may have peace in me. Here on earth you will have many trials and sorrows. But take heart, because I have overcome the world. John 16:33

Then you will experience God's peace, which exceeds anything we can understand. His peace will guard your hearts and minds as you live in Christ Jesus. Philippians 4:7

When that sudden storm hit the lake, the winds started blowing and the waves started filling the boat. The disciples were fearful and thought they were going to drown. They were desperate. Running to Jesus, they found Him sleeping. Two of my favorite words that are often put together in the Bible are, "But God." Previous to this phrase, you can find impossible circumstances or obstacles. Following this phrase, you see that God had a plan all along to bring good about for His people. Time and again, we see these "But God" moments in the scriptures, encouraging us that what we see at first doesn't always dictate our outcome. It's a transitional phrase—a phrase that shifts our focus from the circumstance at hand, to the God who holds us in His hands. In this "suddenly" story of the storm, the phrase, "But Jesus," isn't followed with encouraging words. Like the disciples, we find out that in the middle of their storm, Jesus is sleeping. *Sleeping!* Fear grips them like never before, and the urgency of the situation urges the disciples to wake their savior so they can be saved. When we call on our savior, He is always faithful to answer. While at times He doesn't always answer as quickly as He does in this story, He *will* answer us.

Jesus responded, "Why are you afraid? You have so little faith!" Then he got up and rebuked the wind and waves, and suddenly there was a great calm. The disciples were amazed. "Who is this man?" they asked. "Even the winds and waves obey him!" Matthew 8:26–27

The storm didn't take the disciples out. However, this second "suddenly" surely blew them away. It wasn't just that Jesus calmed a storm, He calmed *their* storm. This experience amazed them. Peace surrounded them. They would never be the same. Just like the power of Jesus bringing peace to their storm amazed the disciples, the peace I felt in that operating room amazed me. Having felt His peace in the middle of the storm, I longed for a steadying peace that would carry me into, through, and out of any storm I would face in life. Though that peace flooded my being in the OR, I still faced moments where fear led my heart to skip a few beats instead of trusting in the One who could bring that calming I needed. I could hear Jesus's question to the disciples echoing in my own heart, "Why are you afraid?"

In our humanness, we all long for control. When circumstances turn to "suddenlies" and we realize we have no control, fear can come in like a flood. Fear gripped me to the core in May 2011, when my heart skipped a couple of beats more than it should have. A feeling of rapid heartbeats came over me and wouldn't let up. As much as I tried to focus on breathing and staying calm, my heart just wouldn't cooperate—peace wouldn't come. A visit to my doctor was in order. Before I knew it, tests were being ordered. My EKG was normal. However, my doctor thought it would be best to follow up with a cardiologist. I ended up leaving the cardiologist's office wearing a heart monitor. I was told to wear it for twenty-four hours. It would monitor my heart's condition and would hopefully give the doctor a clue as to what was going on. How was I supposed to stay calm when my heart was being monitored?

The crazy contraption was annoying to wear, and I was still feeling those palpitations off and on. I was terrified that there would be something wrong with my heart. I experienced the emotional pain of a broken heart, but could it be that my heart was actually broken? The heart is essential, and I needed mine to work. My heart needed to work, not only for myself but for my husband and for my children. Our son was born in 2007 and was a tender four-year-old. Our sweet girl was about to turn eight. My heart couldn't be broken. Wave after wave of "what ifs" kept crashing over the side of my boat. No matter how much I prayed for God's peace, it wasn't calming my racing heart. Was Jesus asleep in the middle of my storm? Surely, He would wake up any moment and calm the waves.

The twenty-four-hour monitor test showed some abnormalities. I was sent to see an electrophysiologist, a cardiac doctor that focuses on the heart's timing, or electrical system. All I knew at this point was I felt like the fear of this storm was sucking the power right out of my heart. The electrophysiologist recommended that I wear another heart monitor for three weeks. It just so happened to coincide with a three-week vacation that we planned to California for the summer. We were going to visit my parents, and my husband would only be able to join us for the last part of our trip. So off I went with the kids on a jet plane. Once we landed and got to my parents' house, I was to start wearing the monitor. The doctor said that at any time the monitor could go off. I was to then call a number, hold the phone to the monitor, and press a button that would register a fax-like sound. This sound wave would send a message to the doctor about what my heart was doing right before the monitor sounded. Those were the hardest three weeks of vacation ever. I had a very hard time relaxing and enjoying time with family and friends because I could literally feel the weight of the situation as the heart monitor hung on my body.

Twice while we were there, the monitor went off. I called in as I was told and then spoke with a nurse who asked me questions about what I was doing and how I was feeling. Both times I was just sitting, and I felt absolutely nothing when the monitor went off. That scared me all the more. If I wasn't able to feel anything, how was I to know the state of my own heart? How would I know if something was really wrong? I guess the doctor would be able to tell me after the monitor test was complete. So, I waited in this boat called life. All the while it seemed I felt nothing but the wind blowing and the waves lapping against me as they filled the boat. That sinking feeling started to mark my days with a fear that gripped me stronger than ever before.

When our summer vacation was over, it was time for a follow-up with the electrophysiologist. He saw some abnormalities of skipped heartbeats on my monitor test results. In order for him to fully diagnose the potential problem, he would need to perform a procedure on me to gain more knowledge. He said I was facing a number of possibilities. It could be that I needed some medication to help my heart. I could possibly need a pacemaker to tell my heart exactly when to beat. Or worst-case scenario, I could need a new heart altogether. I may have been sitting in a chair on dry ground, but at that moment my heart sank under the waves and I just couldn't bear it. The doctor gave me some numbers to call when I got home to schedule the procedure. My husband and I left the doctor's office, and I cried the entire way home.

Later that night, once the kids were in bed, we talked for quite a while. John felt a strong sense of peace in his own heart that I would be okay. He felt it so strongly. He thought I could just trust the Lord myself and not go through with the procedure. "Okay, whatever," I thought, "You can hold onto your faith, but this is my heart and I need to know some real proof that I will be okay." I was not feeling the same sense of peace he was, and since the heart is vital to life, I felt I had no choice but to go through with the procedure.

A few days before the procedure, I remember being gripped with fear. The kids and I just returned home from a trip to the grocery store. I couldn't tell if my heart was skipping beats because there was something broken, or if I was experiencing a bit of panic. As I pulled into the garage, I just leaned over the steering wheel and broke down crying in front of the kids. My sweet girl knew that something was going on with my heart and that I needed to find out how to fix it. This firstborn daughter of mine asked Jesus into her own heart when she was only four years old. Her faith had always been strong, and at that moment she put her hand on my right shoulder and started to pray for me. She trusted that Jesus would be with me through the procedure, and in a moment I will never forget, she prayed these words, "Jesus, you know exactly what Momma needs. It could be a new heart, or it could be a peacemaker. Whatever it is, we trust you will be with her and with us." A peacemaker—a slip of the tongue on her part, but exactly what I needed to hear at that moment. I had the peacemaker with me: Jesus the Prince of Peace! For a few sweet moments, my heart was blanketed with peace, knowing that Jesus really would be with me.

A handful of sleepless nights filled with a pounding heart passed by. September rolled around and the day of the procedure was upon me. I was prepped for the OR and wheeled in. The electrophysiologist who used a lot of big words and technical terms behind his desk ended up having the best bedside manners I have ever experienced. When I met him, I thought he was so cold and matter of fact. My husband thought he was just a really smart doctor who knew his stuff. We trusted he would get the answers we needed through this procedure. His compassion and reassurance that he would be there for me and get those answers were very comforting.

Doctors and nurses do the best job they can in preparing you for what you will face during a procedure. With the waves of fear that were crashing over me leading up to this thing, I didn't quite understand exactly what would happen. Once in the OR, my arms were laid out and strapped down, to keep me from shifting during the procedure. I was literally lying there flat on my back, with my arms stretched out like Jesus on the cross. The nurse started talking to me about what would happen next. They would clean an area at the top of my right leg near the groin and give me a numbing shot. Then the doctor would go in through a cut, place electrodes into my artery, feed them through that artery and attach them onto my heart. Then the test would begin. I asked her when they would be putting me to sleep and she said, "Oh honey, I am sorry if you were mistaken, but you have to be awake during this procedure. If we were to put you under, it would affect the rhythm of your heart and that would not allow us to get accurate test results. Once you are numb, though, you won't feel a thing."

What? Wait a second here…I am going to be awake through this torturous test? Good night! I wanted to jump off the table. The nurse kept telling me to try and remain calm because apparently the blood pressure cuff kept getting a high reading every time it went off. Well, let's just strap you to a table and zap your heart and see how calm you can be. I stared at the ceiling tile above me, praying for peace to come. Once the doctor had the electrodes in place, he told me he was going to start the test and for me to just lay very still. Then he proceeded to leave the room with the rest of the medical team. I was left alone in the room. At first, I thought they must have seen something like a bomb and had to evacuate. Little did I know that they were taking an x-ray of my heart during the test and in order to keep them from the radiation exposure, they had to go into the other room and run the test from the other side of a glass window. It was like I was some kind of radioactive test dummy. One of the nurses asked me if I would like to listen to some music to see if that would help calm me down. I requested they play some oldies. That good, old classic music reminded me of some fun times as a child when my parents would take us to Reno, Nevada, in the summer to see old classic cars roll down the strip. The music started and the old familiar lyrics began playing over the scratchy operating room speakers, "Life would be a dream, if I could take you up to paradise up above." Um, next song, PLEASE!

Y'all, at that point the test started, and my heart was being charged up like Frankenstein and the song was talking about paradise up above. Sweet Jesus, take me now! I knew that any moment I would blink and step into eternity. The nurse kindly skipped to another song. I continued to freak out as my heart was forced to beat rapidly. Following the lead of the disciples, I looked to my savior to save me. I was crying out to Him in my spirit, praying for peace. Praying that He would save my life and let me live. "Jesus, how much faster can my heart beat? How can this not kill me? I need you. I know you see me, but I need you to bring me your peace right now. I am so scared."

Suddenly, in the middle of the worst experience of my life, a stillness came over me from head to toe. My heart was still beating at the speed of light, but it faded into the distance. Jesus started speaking to me. I felt a rush of wind and a separation of my heart, which I was all too aware of, and my spirit. His words spoke through the howling storm, "*This heart of yours is temporary. No matter what happens to this temporary heart, whether you need a medication, a machine, or a new heart, it doesn't affect what happens to your spirit. This, your spirit, is in my hand forever and nothing that happens to you will change that. You are free to walk out of my hands, but nothing can take you out. You are safe in my hands.*"

God stilled the storm, calmed the waves, and he hushed the hurricane winds to only a whisper. Psalm 107:29 The Passion Translation

Storm-calming peace rushed in and quieted *my* storm. My heart was still beating rapidly, but the nurse came on the speaker and said, "Mrs. Baldwin, you're doing great and your blood pressure is finally coming down. Just hold on, we are almost done." If only she knew the experience I just had, she would know why my blood pressure finally went down. The peace that came as Jesus spoke to me brought a steadying to my spirit that I longed for. It was a peace that drove out all fear. I knew beyond a shadow of a doubt that I would be okay. They could tell me the worst-case scenario, but it didn't matter. I knew that I knew I would be okay. In that moment I felt faith rise up in a strength I had not yet known. His overwhelming peace, knowing I was secure in His grip, filled me with a greater measure of faith.

I'm not quite sure how much time had passed—it seemed like only a few minutes. The doctor's voice came over the speaker and said, "Mrs. Baldwin, it looks like your heart skips a beat now and then, but you are recovering on your own. You won't need anything, medicine or otherwise. You are going to be just fine. We will come in and get you unhooked in a few minutes. You did great." Do you know that I didn't even heave a sigh of relief? The relief already came when Jesus spoke His truth to me. I believe that there is a forging to our faith, a forging of our peace to steady us in the storms. Going into that heart procedure, I didn't know if I would be okay. I needed to know it in a tangible way, a gut level, at the core of who I was. I was put to the test, and peace and faith were forged in my spirit. On that table, everything changed. I was on top of a mountain that could never be shaken. I was in the middle of His hand and nothing could take me out. I was amazed at this Jesus who could calm the storm in me in such a powerful way. I would never be the same.

At the end of the day, it was determined that I have something called Wenckebach. It sounds like a disease an Oompa Loompa might have! Thankfully, all of my symptoms went away. Although I feel occasional palpitations, the anxious ponderings faded away as God's peace took its rightful place. While this was not something for which I would have signed up, I would not change a thing. The lesson I learned through this experience can never be taken away from me. I stand in confidence in the promise of God's Word that nothing can take me away from His hand.

From eternity to eternity I am God. No one can snatch anyone out of my hand. No one can undo what I have done. Isaiah 43:13

Beloved, you were knit together in your mother's womb by the Prince of Peace. It is His desire that you walk in peace and not be led by fear. We can rest in Him through the "suddenlies" of life, knowing He will hold us in His hands and that He holds all things together. Be still, beloved, and let His peace still all of your storms.

Be still, and know that I am God. Psalm 46:10

He existed before anything else, and he holds all creation together. Colossians 1:17

Chapter 5

HOPE-FAITH

I t turns out that the valley in which I found myself during my heart situation ended up being a mountaintop experience in the end. I have heard it said that the Kingdom of God is a bit upside down compared to the ways of this world. The Bible tells us it's better if we give than if we receive. We are advised to lose our life if we want to gain it. God blesses the poor in spirit, the meek, the widows, and orphans. Things that are not given much value by worldly standards are highly valued by the King of Heaven. So, when your life seems a bit upside down, maybe it's that way because your valley is really a mountaintop. After my experience on that operating room table, I sure felt like the whole of my situation flipped and I was standing tall on a God mountain, filled with peace and faith like never before. It was a pivotal moment and a catalyst for changing the way I thought about anything I would face in the future. I was firmly grounded in Christ and assured that nothing could snatch me from His hands.

When we climb a mountain in the natural world, it takes all our strength to press on to the top. We are cautious about the placement of each grip of our hands and step of our feet. The going may be slow and steady. There will be times of needed rest and refreshment along the way. The same can be said of our journey back down the mountain. We see from a new perspective, take in the glory of a mountaintop vista, and we are filled with awe and wonder as we make our way back down. We have to continue to be careful where we place our feet. Our secure footing on the way down is vital. We cannot allow the glory of the vistas of the past blind us to what comes our way. And so it is along life's journey. We take in the mountaintop vista, treasuring the victory of the climb. We own the stories we have walked through. We must place any new challenge next to the truth through which we have walked. We walk forward in the confidence of our testimony, not allowing new challenges to slip us up.

On the heels of my heart procedure, the fall season brought on a terrible head cold with pain, pressure, and congestion like I had never seen. Doctors couldn't figure out why. After a few rounds of antibiotics and steroids, my symptoms were not improving. All I knew is that I would have given anything for some type of miracle treatment where they could remove my head, decongest it, and then return it to me when all was well. The pain was getting worse and I just wanted to feel better. Soon an MRI was ordered, and the waiting game began. Waiting for results can be a truly stressful time, but after my heart experience in September, I was able to wait in peace. I knew that whatever the test results showed, I would be okay in God's hand. The tests revealed that I needed to have sinus surgery to remove large polyps that were causing all that pain and pressure. As much as I love the beauty of nature on the East Coast of this great country of ours, I can honestly say I am allergic to it. We lived on the East Coast for almost ten years and my sinuses were always in overdrive. Apparently, my body built up these polyps as a way to fight against pollen entering my sinuses. After a few months of suffering, I had sinus surgery in early 2012 and faced it in complete peace. Sure, there was a bit of the unknown and normal apprehension of facing surgery, but at the core of who I was, I was able to face the unknown in total peace. I was walking in the confidence of my testimony, and it was so refreshing.

Sinus surgery was successful. It took about six weeks to fully heal. I was feeling less and less congestion and pressure as the weeks went on. At some point during the spring, I was released to full activity and sent on my way. With the snow melting and flowers blooming, it was a great time to breathe deeply the fresh air. Springtime in the Northeast is a beautiful time of year. After the harsh winter melts away, new life starts to emerge. I will never forget the first spring we experienced in New Jersey. It felt like the glorious rebirth of the earth. When the spring showers weren't falling, my son and I would enjoy long walks through the Turtle Back Zoo. He loved to ride the little train, and we would take in the wonder of the trees as they unfurled their green leaves. So many different shades of green filled the trees above. It was becoming my favorite time of year.

Finally pain-free, I was able to really enjoy the days with my son while my oldest daughter was in school. My son celebrated his fifth birthday in early April. He was full of life and questions. He was excited about starting kindergarten in the fall and loved to do preschool workbooks at home with me. He just completed one, and so off to the store we went in search of a new one. With our shopping finished, we buckled into the car for the ride home. It was then that he asked me *the* question. "Mommy, how does a baby get into a mommy's tummy?" Those are the kind of questions that can activate this momma's Wenchkebach! No, really, your heart starts to beat a little faster when the little ones of your life ask such questions.

I said a quick prayer to Jesus, asking for the right words to answer his honest question. My answer went something like this: "Well, once you get married, you are allowed to do something very special with your spouse, which you will learn about when you are older. You and your spouse can do this special thing together as often as you like and nothing will come of it. However, when God decides to start knitting a baby together, He makes a spark of life happen in the mommy's tummy when the parents share their special moment together. After that, the baby starts growing, and in about nine months the baby is born." His response was as simple as his question, "Okay. Thanks, Mommy." And with that I drove us home pondering his question in my heart. During Easter service at church just a few days earlier, on April 8, 2012, I heard God's voice whispering to me, *"You will be pregnant before this summer."* Although it was written in my journal, I hadn't told a soul.

On April 24, 2012, I found out I was pregnant with our third child. Immediately, I was filled with awe, wonder, and joy. About a year and a half prior to this expectant news, John and I were a bit discouraged. We tried to get pregnant, hoping to expand our family and have another child. It just wasn't happening, and we began to wonder if a third child was part of God's plan for our family. We started praying about the possibility of adopting. We attended an informational meeting regarding adoption at a local Christian adoption agency. Before we were married, John and I talked about our heart for having children. We were open to adopting if it turned out we were unable to have our own children. With the heart to grow our family and the information of adoption in hand, we had a lot to think about. On the drive home that evening, John and I both had a feeling that we were not to adopt at that time. It was as if God was saying to wait. The following Sunday at church, there was a prophetic word spoken before the prayer ministry time. A person from the prayer team said, "We heard God say that there is a couple here that is hoping to have another baby and has even looked into adopting. God wants you to know that He has a baby for you from your own womb and to trust Him with the timing. If you feel that word is for you, please come up for prayer." WOW.

Needless to say, John and I practically ran up for prayer. The person who prayed for us was the prayer team member that received the word from the Lord. She prayed over us and encouraged us to wait on Him for His perfect timing. That settled it. When God speaks, we listen and obey. We walked away filled with excitement and expectation that we would, in God's time, indeed be expecting. Time went on, and on, and on. At some point, although I was given a new measure of faith, I decided that God was taking His sweet time and I wasn't getting any younger. It wasn't that I didn't believe in His promise to us for a baby; I just kind of stopped thinking about it. In fact, in March 2012, I decided to do some early spring cleaning. I gathered up baby toys and items we no longer needed for a donation. I figured that if God did bless us with another baby at some point, then He would provide for all we needed at that time. In the meantime, the baby stuff was becoming a bit of a sore spot, a reminder of a promise not yet fulfilled. Sometimes we are quick to give up, or we hold loosely to the promise God gives us. A few weeks after donating the baby items, God's promise came to pass. He indeed was knitting together His promised baby in my womb, in His perfect timing. In an amazing miraculous turn of events, I realized I indeed conceived this baby the weekend of Easter. The same weekend I heard the Lord whisper to me that I would be pregnant before the summer!

John and I were filled with excitement, and the children were beside themselves with the news that a new sibling would soon be joining our family. We were quick to share the news with family and friends. I was literally glowing with joy. The school year came to an end and I was really looking forward to a wonderful summer. I am both blessed and thankful to be a stay-at-home mom. Once my oldest daughter started school, the highlight of my year became summer vacation. Those sandcastle, bucket-filled days of fun together with my children are treasured moments I will hold dear for all my life. We knew this summer would be a bit different, as it would be filled with a handful of doctor visits for the new baby and me. If I had a doctor visit, usually the kids tagged along with me. It was hard to find a sitter during the middle of the day. On June 21,

2012, at twelve weeks and one-day gestation, the kids joined me for an in-depth ultrasound appointment.

The children were settled yet wiggling with excitement as they sat next to me looking at a big screen waiting to see their baby sibling via the ultrasound. The technician dimmed the lights and began. Before long, through the blurs and blobs, Pebble came into view. You see, John and I chose to give all of our children womb names. We enjoyed the element of surprise in not finding out the gender of our children until they were born. Our oldest daughter went by "Peanut," and our son went by "Puzzle." We figured we had to stick with the "P" theme and chose the womb name of Pebble for our third baby. The technician was pretty quiet as she proceeded with the ultrasound. The kids and I were in awe at this little life growing inside me. At twelve weeks gestation, the average baby will be about two inches in length and weigh about half an ounce. The technician paused the ultrasound and mentioned that the doctor would be coming in for a closer look. I thought nothing of it as the kids and I talked about how cute Pebble was. The joy on their faces was priceless.

When the door to my exam room opened, the technician entered along with one of the perinatal doctors. The doctor introduced himself to me and then told me he wanted to "take a closer look at this fetus." He focused on the backside of Pebble's neck and started talking about a sack of fluid and something wrong. Tears began to fill my eyes. A hush fell over the room. My heart began to beat faster as the doctor proceeded to explain that there was something called a cystic hygroma, something about too much fluid, something about a negative outlook, something about. . . his voice seemed to fade for a moment as my world came to a halt. The next thing I remember was the doctor saying, "My advice would be to abort." The clear picture of my sweet baby Pebble became blurred by the tears now slowly flowing from my eyes. At the same time, something came over me—a boldness. The Spirit of God was giving me strength and peace in the middle of yet another sudden moment. I interrupted the doctor and told him to stop talking for a minute. I asked the technician to please take my children out into the hallway so the doctor and I could speak without them having to hear anything further. The joy that was in my children's eyes moments before was now replaced with a fearful, questioning look.

As soon as the children were out of the room, the boldness of the Spirit of God literally spoke through me. Through tears, I told the doctor, "All I know is that God is fearfully and wonderfully knitting this baby together in my womb and I am going to have faith in His Word over yours. Abortion is not an option. This child is a gift from God to me, and I will take the gift that he is giving me."

For you created my inmost being; you knit me together in my mother's womb. I praise you because I am fearfully and wonderfully made; your works are wonderful, I know that full well. Psalm 139:13–14 NIV

All I knew at that moment was the Spirit of God spoke the Word of God out of the depth of my spirit. The truth of the moment for me and my baby was that God was the one knitting this baby together and that is the word in which I chose to hear, believe, and have faith. The Word of God will stand forever, and I knew at a gut level I could trust God's Word over the words of this practicing doctor. I would indeed put my faith in God, the Great Physician, but the battle for this baby would be fierce.

The doctor continued to give me statistics. With everything they were seeing on the screen, there was a 90 percent chance this "fetus" would have a severe chromosomal defect. Most likely the "fetus" wouldn't even make it full term and the pregnancy would likely end in a miscarriage. If by chance the "fetus" made it to full term, there was a "95 percent likelihood of a short-term pediatric outcome." The baby would have a very high chance of dying anywhere from moments after the birth up to the first year. There could be disfigurement that would be a scary thing for my young children to see in a sibling. That could cause them unnecessary trauma. The best advice this doctor gave was abortion. The best thing he could advise me to do was to kill this baby who God clearly promised to give us. I reiterated the fact that nothing he could say would change my mind on abortion.

It felt like the world truly stopped spinning. John and I had always been pro-life. For years, we supported a variety of biblically based crisis pregnancy centers. These safe harbors to moms facing an unplanned pregnancy were something about which we became very passionate. The truth is that abortion isn't a woman's only option. There are people in this world who would love to come alongside a woman facing an unplanned pregnancy and see her through, support her with resources and counseling, and give her the tools to care for her baby after birth. There are actual options, and a baby doesn't mean your life has to come to a halt. When you have a voice in a cause, put your money where your mouth is in support of that cause. It becomes a powerful force for good in the world. The enemy will find any sneaky way he can to slither in and pin you against what you are against. Never in my entire life would I have thought I would be facing the option of abortion. Never did I think I would be faced with the moment of choice, or asked the question, "Would you like to abort?" Yet here I was and there was no question about it. I would never end a life that God began. He is the Author and Finisher and I would choose, we would choose, to leave the knitting of our promised baby in His Almighty capable hands.

With my own questions swirling around and a bit of a numb feeling hitting me in the womb, I continued the conversation with the doctor. He informed me that there were a variety of tests they could run that would help them to figure out exactly what type of chromosomal issue we may be facing. In an effort to give this baby the best chance of survival, I declined to have any invasive testing.

I would not agree to anything that would increase a chance for miscarriage. At the end of the day, I decided that they could take a round of bloodwork and send it off to the lab for testing. There were a few things they could find out from those tests, and it was all I was willing to do. Needless to say, the doctor thought I was a crazy person and that I would eventually come around. He said he "respected my decision," yet reminded me of the time limits of pregnancy termination in the state of New Jersey (just in case). I told the doctor that I appreciated his authority in the medical field and all of the hours and money he poured into becoming who he was. However, I was going to trust God on this. He left a handful of papers on the counter for me to take on my way out. He told me I would be followed very closely via ultrasounds throughout my pregnancy and to follow up with the genetic counselor. He spoke coldly as a man of science and medicine and left me alone in the cold exam room. As I finished changing and gathered my papers, I realized I had a lot of thoughts to collect as well. I just wanted to run home and fall into my husband's arms and cry out to God, "WHY?" I entered the hallway and saw my two precious gifts from God waiting for me with the technician. With tears gently falling, I embraced them and held on with all my might. I knew they were scared and confused, and I assured them we would talk about it on the way home. I just had to find the strength to walk to the counter, make my next appointment, and drive us home. Somehow, I did just that.

On our short drive home, I explained to the kids that the doctors were concerned with some extra fluid at the back of Pebble's neck. My tender children were only nine and five. My momma-heart wanted to just tuck them away somewhere safe so they didn't have to hear any of this. At the same time, I have always been more honest with my children than some parents. I hated that the doctor actually recommended abortion in front of my children. My daughter knew what it meant, and she knew her daddy and I would never make that decision. I decided to tell my son that sometimes people decide to end the life of the baby because the baby is really sick. His opinion on the matter was, "That is really very sad, Mommy." I told them I was so sorry they had to hear the doctor say scary things about their baby sibling. When we got home, we prayed together, and I told the kids that daddy and I would be trusting God to knit this baby together in my womb. I thought it was very sweet that just weeks before this happened, I used the very same verse to explain to my son how a baby gets into a mommy's tummy. While the kids were filled with childlike faith that God would do a good job, they were also in a realm of the unknown right along with John and me.

That afternoon I sent off a quick email to family and friends asking for prayers for our sweet baby and our little family. The kids were playing in the basement, and I sat in the recliner looking out the window waiting for my husband to come home. My OBGYN actually called me to check in and see how I was doing. She received a call about my ultrasound screening results and wanted to make sure I was okay. This sweet doctor of mine actually offered to meet me for coffee if I needed to just talk, as her shift was ending soon. I was blown away by her compassion, but during our conversation I realized that she thought there wasn't a good chance for the baby to survive. It was then that I surprised not only the doctor but myself right along with her. I said, "I truly believe this baby is a gift from God to my husband and me. Whether I get to hold Pebble here on earth for moments or years, or whether I hold Pebble someday in heaven, the truth is that Pebble is my gift and I will hold him or her in God's perfect timing." My doctor was blown away by my faith and said I would be stronger on the other side of this. She assured me that she would be by my side to see this through, however it turned out. While she shared her own concerns, she also respected my choice and was willing to be by my side. I was thankful for her encouragement.

Later that night, with the kids tucked into bed, John and I lay in our own bed with a deep sadness that hung like thick fog in the room. It doesn't matter if your baby is in the womb attached by an umbilical cord, or out in the world attached to your heartstrings, no parent wants anything to be wrong with their child. While we knew that God spoke His word-promise over Pebble's life and right out of my vocal cords, we were flooded with the unknown and what-ifs that swirled at us. All we could do was place our trust in the God who promised this baby to us in the first place. We could trust that the prayers of family and friends would help hold us together as we held on to each other. We tucked trust, hope, and faith in God's Word into our hearts and fell asleep with tear-stained pillows.

On July 3, I went for a follow-up ultrasound. Thankfully, I was able to find a sitter for the kids and my husband was able to join me for this visit. The perinatal office we visited had seven doctors that took care of ultrasounds. I was on course to see just about every single one of them. We met a new doctor at this visit, and he was pretty quiet as the ultrasound began. Finally, he spoke. "The nuchal cystic hygroma has decreased in size, but it is still a big concern. I am also noticing a Reversed A wave of the ductus venosus waveform." In simple terms, the heart was working abnormally. That combined with the amount of fluid in the nuchal cystic hygroma made the doctor believe there was a very high risk of a chromosomal abnormality. My previous blood test results hadn't come in yet, so they couldn't know anything for sure. After the ultrasound, we found ourselves sitting on the other side of the doctor's desk having a discussion. The doctor reiterated what had been told to us prior, that most likely this baby wouldn't make it. We were reminded of the term limits on abortion in the state. We reiterated our decision to keep this baby and trust God with the outcome. Faith in God doesn't seem to be easy for some doctors. I can respect their point of view and I just wished they would not continue to bring up all the negative. This doctor strongly felt that

Pebble would most likely have Down syndrome. He knew that we had a trip planned to California to visit family, and he suggested we stay in close proximity to a hospital at all times. He suggested that we notify the flight crew that I was a high-risk pregnancy and could miscarry at any moment. Doom, doom, doom. It just felt like the doctor had nothing but death and doom to declare over our sweet little Pebble. It was heartbreaking news, to say the least. With our follow-up ultrasound scheduled, we left the meeting blanketed in sadness.

Although we were trusting in the Lord, the truth of the facts presented to us brought deep sadness. I knew that I could trust in the Lord, but I also didn't fully know how this whole thing would play out. I remember crying quietly on the way home. Once home, I sent off another email update to family and friends. I was so thankful for the slight good news that the fluid level of the nuchal cystic hygroma had gone down. That had to be a praise report, right? But then, there was also a new prayer request regarding the heart not working properly. Thankful for family and friends who would be faithful to lift up our arms in the battle over our baby, I signed off my email and tried to focus. It was so very hard to just do everyday life with this huge heaviness blanketing us. John and I spent a lot of time just holding onto each other. There were many silent moments. We could only be still and trust the Lord. We had to remind our kids that God was in control of Pebble's life and in that, remind ourselves as well.

On July 5, I received a call from the genetic counselor who had the results of my blood work. This blood work was looking for Trisomy 21, 18, and 13. These are three major chromosomal defects. Trisomy 21 is Down syndrome and the other two syndromes would be worst-case scenarios with very little hope for a good outcome. Our prayers up to this point were that this test would come back negative for all three. We were not opposed to having a Down syndrome baby, but our hearts' desire was a healthy baby with no abnormalities. If the test turned out positive, we would use that information to prepare in how to care for the baby. My palms were so sweaty as the counselor began going over the results that I thought the phone would slip to the floor. In my heart, I was saying a prayer, "Lord, this baby was your promise to us, and I trust you with whatever these results say. Have your way, Jesus." The genetic counselor proceeded to inform me that the test for Trisomy 21, 18, and 13 all came back negative. My heart was screaming, "Thank you, Jesus!" I was then asked if I would like to know the gender of the baby. My husband and I had a hunch that with these results we might be able to find out the gender, and with all the unknowns we decided that this time around we wanted to know. It turned out that the blood work showed only X chromosomes, so Pebble was a girl! The genetic counselor said that her guess was that if there was a chromosomal disorder, this baby may have something called Turner's syndrome. Turner's syndrome is something that only affects females and it means they are missing an X chromosome, having only one instead of two. Symptoms can range from vital organ issues, short stature, fertility issues, and learning disabilities, among other things. However, this is a much more favorable chromosomal defect than the other three. The doctors wouldn't be able to know anything for sure without the invasive testing, but I felt comfortable waiting until Pebble was born to find out.

I was very encouraged by the news from this test result. The doctors continued to be very cautious with leaning toward any optimism. As frustrating as it was to hear negative news throughout this pregnancy, I know it was frustrating for the doctors to wait for Pebble's birth to really know what was going on. The doctors were waiting on Pebble and we were waiting on God. In the waiting, we were able to enjoy a trip to California over the summer. It was a relief knowing some good news going into our trip as it let us enjoy our time together with family and friends without the looming results hanging over us. We were excited to know that our sweet, promised baby was a girl, and the name selection process began. John, the kids, and I were starting to get excited, but there was still the unknown outcome ahead of us.

As August rolled around, John and I celebrated ten years of marriage. Our children were getting ready to head back to school and the summer days were coming to an end. My daughter would be entering fourth grade and my son would be starting kindergarten. It was a big year for all of us. The kids enrolled in a private Christian school for the first time, and I drove forty minutes one way to get them there. The mornings came early, and the days were long. Mid-August, I had another ultrasound and the doctor reported that there was a "slight remnant of the cystic hygroma in the sagittal plane only. The nuchal fold was normal. The ductus venosus showed a smaller than expected A wave, but it was much improved over the reversal of A-wave previously noted." The doctor actually said he was cautiously optimistic! I would need to follow up with a pediatric cardiologist to get a closer look at Pebble's heart, but John and I were overjoyed to hear such great news. The fluid at the back of Pebble's neck was almost completely gone, and things were improving with her heart. She literally went from a Down syndrome type of heartbeat to a normal one, and this was a huge answer to prayer. The doctors were baffled as to how all of this could have reversed on its own. We knew it was God who was in control.

My days were long with the commute to the kid's school and all the many doctor visits. It was one of the most exhausting seasons of my life. The pediatric cardiologist wasn't able to see Pebble's heart very well at all. Every time we went in for an ultrasound at his office, the baby would be hiding under my belly button area. One time her arms were even crossed over her heart. It was as if she wanted to be left alone. The fact that her arms made the shape of a cross over her heart was something that brought a smile to my own heart. I felt more and more confident that this baby would be okay—that God would indeed work a miracle and give us a healthy baby girl. There were some doctors at the perinatal ultrasound office who were still very negative and frustrated with the unknown factor of this pregnancy. I just reassured them that no matter what happened, we would be thankful for the gift this baby was to us and we would continue trusting the Lord. During this season, so many of our friends and family members would comment on how they were encouraged by my strong faith. Can I tell you that it was only the strength of God in me? The struggle of this whole situation was so heavy and real. There was still a chance that something could be wrong, and we just wouldn't know until we knew. The waiting was very difficult. There were days where fear would come against me and I could almost hear the enemy of my soul whisper his lies into my ear, things like, "You shouldn't even buy a car seat because you won't be needing it after all." In those real and raw spiritual battle moments, I would feel the haunting of hopes being dashed.

I remember one day, the particular doctor who did my ultrasound was very negative and gloomy with his outlook. I came away feeling so discouraged. As I mentioned in the introduction of this book, I decided to call Mom. No trauma of the past could have stopped me from needing to hear her voice that day. Throughout the years, I had been faithful to call my parents to update them on our lives, especially their grandchildren. My dad lived to hear my voice on the phone but wasn't one to talk much after his stroke. He still had the ability, but he had become more withdrawn. I placed that call to Mom and filled her in as tears spilled down my cheeks. I remember telling her about writing a book one day and calling it *Hopes Dashed*. That was when she prayed for my perspective to be changed—or Jesus to change my heart. That was the day I read the sweet words that flooded my soul and my situation with hope like no other.

Sustain me, my God, according to your promises, and I will live; do not let my hopes be dashed. Psalm 119:116 NIV

That was it. It was no strength of my own. It was God and His promises that were helping me to live through this pregnancy. He wasn't only changing my perspective on hope and this very book's title, He was telling me I would not have my hopes of a healthy baby be dashed. I knew at that moment it would be okay, but reminders would be needed. I was so weak, yet He remained strong!

Each time he said, "My grace is all you need. My power works best in weakness." So now I am glad to boast about my weaknesses, so that the power of Christ can work through me. 2 Corinthians 12:9

In October, while we were in the middle of our own pregnancy storm of the unknown, it was well known that a hurricane was heading our way. Superstorm Sandy made its mark on the Northeast, and we hunkered down in the basement the night the storm came ashore. The kids were a bit scared but excited at the same time. We had a family sleepover in the basement of our townhome. The kids slept on an air mattress and John and I were in the guest bed. We lost power at some point in the evening, and the kids and John were able to fall fast asleep, while I lay wide awake. I remember looking out the small basement window and I could see the sky light up with both lightning and the glow power line transformers make as they fail and sparks fly. I remember thinking that this superstorm was like a natural representation of what I was going through emotionally and spiritually in my pregnancy. I didn't know what we would wake up to the next morning. I didn't know what I would wake up to once Pebble's life dawned on the earth. What I did know is that my God would be with me. He would be just as powerful through the storm as well as the aftermath of the storm. And He was faithfully keeping me in His perfect peace.

You will keep in perfect peace all who trust in you, all whose thoughts are fixed on you! Isaiah 26:3

When you go through deep water, I will be with you. When you go through rivers of difficulty, you will not drown. When you walk through the fire of oppression, you will not be burned up; the flames will not consume you. Isaiah 43:2

We survived the hurricane fairly well. We lost power for about five days, which was no fun with two young children and a pregnant momma. My husband had long commutes as the roads were a total mess. We had no damage to our townhome, and eventually life started to return to normal, even though for many in the Northeast, it was a very different normal. The doctors were still closely watching me and anxiously awaiting Pebble's arrival. Over the course of my pregnancy, I had over twenty-five ultrasounds to monitor the baby's health. About a month before Pebble arrived, I was informed that I had a two-vessel umbilical cord. A normal umbilical cord has three vessels, two arteries and one vein. My umbilical cord had one vein and one artery. About one percent of pregnancies will have a two-vessel umbilical cord. While it isn't a severe issue, it is usually present in babies that are smaller in size. For some reason, this news just really bummed me out. I felt deflated and that it was a sign that there may indeed be something wrong with Pebble. Maybe she would have Turner's syndrome after all. I was feeling desperate for a reminder of the promise of God.

On November 18, 2012, during worship on a Sunday morning, I remember asking Jesus to help steady my wandering heart. I needed some encouragement to get me through this pregnancy. I needed a strong reminder of His promise. I was given another picture. I saw a willow tree in a green pasture near a lake surrounded by evergreen trees. As I looked at the beautiful willow tree, I saw Jesus walk out from behind it. In my spirit, I knew He had a gift to present to me. I could see Jesus holding Pebble in a cozy, pink knitted blanket. She was beautiful and healthy and the look in His eyes was so peaceful. I felt Him saying, *"This is my child in whom I delight and love, just as I delight in you and love you. This is my promise to you and my gift to you. You can trust me and my promise over what the doctors are saying. She is safe and secure in my arms and will be in your arms in my timing, you can trust in me."*

I cannot express into words the immense feeling of delight that swept over me as I saw that picture. Jesus loves you so much, beloved, and you are His greatest delight. As I sat there writing like crazy in my journal of the picture I was given, I knew I wanted to add a special middle name to our promised daughter's name. The meaning of a name has always been important to John and me. We cared about the biblical meaning and story behind each name. We also wanted our children's names to play a part in their story. With this daughter, we knew that her name needed to reflect that she was promised to us by the Lord. We knew that His grace was sufficient during the waiting. We knew that the Lord delighted in her.

My water broke at 5:00 a.m. on December 26, 2012. Just the day before, we were celebrating the miraculous birth of our Lord and Savior, Jesus Christ—the one we put first above the doctor's reports. When I realized it was actually my water breaking, I woke John up and told him we forgot to open one present. He jumped out of bed and we raced to the hospital. It just so happened that the first C-section of the morning was canceled, and I was given that spot because I arrived so early. At 8:32 a.m., Bella Tirzah Grace entered the world. She weighed in at five pounds, eight ounces and was seventeen inches long. While she was the smallest of our three children, she was healthy and perfect. It would take a handful of months to confirm, but blood tests finally came back showing that Bella was indeed perfectly healthy. All of her chromosomes are right where they need to be—nothing doubled, nothing missing. Bella had no defects. What she did have was a beautiful story of God's miraculous touch on her life in the womb, a family who was over the moon with joy at the outcome, an extended family and many friends who rejoiced at the news of her healthy delivery, and a God who was faithful to His promised Word, who gets all the glory, and who loves her very much. Bella also had one sweet detail that we never expected but blew the doctors out of the water. On her forehead was a birthmark that is commonly referred to as an Angel's Kiss.

The name Bella was chosen from the Hebrew name Isabella meaning: the promise of God or God is my oath.

The name Tirzah is Hebrew for: she is my delight.

The name Grace means: God is gracious, or God's favor.

Through this storm, I learned firsthand that God keeps His promises. His *Word* is faithful and true. I had faith in God and His promise, and it was a beautiful thing. At the same time, I want to say that I believe there is a great mystery to the Kingdom of God. There is the *already*: what Christ did on the cross. And there is the *not yet*: the fullness of His Kingdom that is still to come. We live in the tension of that. He is a Sovereign God, and while what we face makes us question, we can never truly question Him, for He stands alone as King of kings and Lord of lords. I know that His Word does not go out and return void. It does what it purposes to do, every single time. In this pregnancy, the Spirit of God declared the Word of God over what the doctor's words were saying. There may be times where you have faced something and declared God's Word over a situation and it doesn't turn out favorable at all. I would encourage you to seek God first in all you do and in all you face. Ask for Him to speak His Word into your circumstances and then trust that. When you know for sure it's the Spirit of God speaking the Word of God to your situation, you can know full well that it will be as He said. Then you can join me in the wondrous journey of hope in faith.

You are blessed because you believed that the Lord would do what he said. Luke 1:45

Chapter 6

HOPE-FOUND

G rowing up, every school I attended had a lost and found—
that area on campus where items were stored as they waited
to be found by their true owner. They were items that were lost yet
found. Even while those items are still lost to the owner, they have
been found by a stranger. What a concept to ponder: that something can be both lost and found at the same time. John Newton
penned undoubtedly the most famous hymn of all time: "Amazing
Grace." In this timeless hymn, he wrote, *"I once was lost, but now
am found."*[2] When the truth of that statement sinks into your soul,
you will never be the same.

I remember all too well that feeling of being a lost little girl.
When Jesus found me with His love through the Miranda family,
it changed everything for me. The truth was that I was found in
the Beloved—Jesus. I was His and He was mine. No matter what
happened in my life, from that moment forward, I knew I belonged
to Jesus forever. I am a firm believer that what God does in you,
He then wants to do through you for the good of others. Little
did I know that one day I would partner with God to find a little

---

[2] Newton, "Amazing Grace."

Ethiopian boy with the love of Jesus, just as the Miranda family did for me.

Early in our marriage, John and I made the decision to sponsor a child through an organization called One Child. The picture of our Ethiopian boy was placed in a frame and displayed so we would see him daily and pray for him and his family. Our monthly donation provided him with an education, a hot meal at school, and the chance to hear about the love of Jesus. Through the years, we exchanged letters back and forth. That dream of being a pen pal with someone on the other side of the world became all too real. To be honest, although I prayed for our Ethiopian boy, I didn't write him near as often as he wrote me. That all changed in 2014 when I had a chance to travel to Africa and meet him in person.

On January 12, 2010, Haiti was struck by a catastrophic magnitude 7.0 earthquake. Billions of dollars in damages were nothing compared to the loss of life. Well over 100,000 souls were wiped off the face of the earth. We were moved with compassion to do something to help. We decided to financially support Convoy of Hope. This organization had been feeding children in Haiti since 2007. Their warehouse had just been fully stocked right before the 2010 earthquake hit, and they were positioned to be the hands and feet of Jesus in the aftermath of devastation. I was familiar with Convoy of Hope from my youth group days in high school. This organization was founded by the Donaldson family in 1994. I remember getting up early on a Saturday, riding the church bus about an hour to Sacramento, and passing out bags of groceries in low-income neighborhoods. Blessing others with a tangible gift that would nourish their bodies and bring hope to their souls tethered my heart to heaven. My heart's capacity to see others grew tremendously, and I was so thankful for those times of outreach.

Over the years of supporting Convoy of Hope, we heard wonderful reports of the many ways they were feeding children, empowering women and farmers, and responding to disasters all over the world. Our love for the organization grew all the more. We were blessed to be in a season where we could give in extravagant ways at the time, and it afforded me the opportunity to travel with Convoy of Hope to Ethiopia. I signed up for the trip, began filling out paperwork, and getting vaccines ahead of my travel. A few months before the trip, the connection finally hit me. I was going to *Ethiopia*—the same African country where our sponsor child lived. The wheels started turning and the next thing you know I was on the phone with One Child asking if it would be possible to meet our child. I had no idea how big of a country it was, or if our child would be anywhere near where I was going to be staying, but I had to find out. The One Child representative put me on hold to look at our sponsor child's file. When they came back on the phone, I found out that our child lived in the same area I would be visiting. They began making arrangements for me to meet our Ethiopian son, and I began rearranging my travel so I could arrive a day early for our visit.

My original travel plans were to fly from New York to Washington, DC. I was then to join the Ethiopia Hope Experience team for our trip to Ethiopia. The change to my plans meant I would now be traveling to Ethiopia alone. Almost twenty years before this trip, at the altar one night during the youth group, I felt God say to me, *"You will be going to Africa."* At the time, everything in me was ready to go right then and there. I would have boarded the plane immediately if it were to have landed in the parking lot to pick me up. Little did I know how different God's timing would be. Little did I know that God wanted me to experience handing out groceries to the poor of my own country with an organization that needed to grow up, as did I, in order for me to be able to travel with them to the great continent of Africa.

As the trip came near, I became a bit anxious to travel so far from home, alone. Was I grown up enough to do this? Up until this point, I had driven into Canada for a couple of hours during a trip to Washington state and flown to Mexico a couple of times. Not once had I been on a different continent or had to fly over such a huge body of water. As nervous as I was to go, nothing was going to stop me. One evening about a week before my trip, my son shared his own fears regarding my travel.

"Mommy, I am scared for you to be so far away from me when you are in Africa," Evan said. "There will be a huge ocean between us, and you won't even be on the same continent."

I said a quick prayer, asking God how I should respond to my son in a way that would bring him peace about the distance that would be between us. He is so faithful to be that ever-ready present help in time of need. His response poured out of me.

"Well, Evan, do you know that song we sing about God and how He has the whole world in His hands? When you get nervous about me being so far away from you, remember that song. You will find that you are on one part of the earth and I am over on the other side. The earth, and us on it, will be right in the middle of God's hands. So we will be together after all, even though there will be a bit of distance between us."

To that Evan replied, "Okay, Mommy. Thanks." And with a big hug he bounded off to play with his toys. It's amazing how God brought immediate peace to my son, as well as myself at that moment. What He spoke through me to comfort my own child brought comfort to me as well. Those words would be something I remembered throughout my trip. When I am found in the hands of God, nothing can shake me. Not only did I have the words God spoke through me as a source of comfort, but I also had some verses from the Word of God. These verses fueled my soul as I traveled and learned things only stepping upon African soil could teach me.

Your hands made me and formed me; give me understanding to learn your commands. Psalm 119:73 NIV

For he will order his angels to protect you wherever you go.
Psalm 91:11

We are therefore Christ's ambassadors, as though God were making his appeal through us. We implore you on Christ's behalf: Be reconciled to God. 2 Corinthians 5:20 NIV

The day finally arrived. With the confidence in God's Word that He indeed would order His angels to protect me, I boarded my flight and eventually landed safely in Addis Ababa, Ethiopia, Africa. The first thing I remember was how much the land reminded me of home. The East Bay hills around Oakland, California, are filled with eucalyptus trees, as was Addis Ababa. To this day, the eucalyptus trees sprinkled around the Bay Area take me back to my moments in Ethiopia.

After a light meal, a shower, and a bit of rest in my room, the time had come for me to go visit our sponsored child. I traveled with two companions who were able to translate for me. The roads were jammed with cars. There were no stoplights. Animals of all kinds and car accidents were everywhere. The red dirt blew around in a dust cloud of abundance as we arrived at the school where our sponsor child attended. The corrugated metal gate opened, and I saw him right away. He was only nine years old when we began sponsoring him. Now nineteen years old, grown and tall, he stood before me in person holding a gift. A bouquet of the most beautiful fire-orange roses with golden glitter sprinkled on them. He handed me the roses with shyness, yet his eyes were filled with love and thankfulness words cannot express. We embraced in a hug I will never forget and began a tour of the school. I saw a room filled with children all wide-eyed at the sight of me. All smiling, thriving, and getting a better chance at this journey of life simply because others around the globe like me chose to sponsor each of them. We stopped in the office and I was shown a folder belonging to my sponsor child. It held all the letters and photos that we exchanged over the years. At this point our sponsor child was in tenth grade, healthy, and had a heart filled with the love of God. Our choice to sponsor him almost eleven years earlier provided him the opportunity to be found. No longer lost, but a child of God.

As we exited the office, my Ethiopian son's younger brother came running to him. He gave me a big hug. Oh, the joy that flooded my heart. I was already feeling as if I could burst, and the interpreter informed me that we were going to follow the boys home, where I would get to meet their mother. A teacher gave the boys a ride home, and we followed behind in our car. I will never forget the look of the boys' eyes peering through the window, watching our car following them the whole way, desperate to make sure we didn't get lost.

After a handful of minutes, we arrived at their home. A rocky dirt road with a cluster of earthen-walled homes topped with corrugated metal roofing met us. The narrow path between homes took us past roaming chickens, dogs, and the pile of hay that served as a toilet with not much in the way of privacy. The small front door to their home opened in a big way. For that door opened my heart to love more deeply. As we entered his home, there was a small couch, table, dresser, and even a little TV in the corner. The floors were the very earth, and there was one light bulb in the middle of the ceiling. The earthen walls were painted a bright yellow, like the pollen of a daisy. This small two-roomed home had *big* things inside. Big love, hope, dignity, gratitude, hugs, tears, and smiles—smiles bigger than the sky and brighter than the sun.

Then this Ethiopian son of mine introduced me to his mother. We embraced and cried tears of joy together. She brewed us coffee over hot coals and served nuts and popcorn. The hospitality was overwhelming. Our Ethiopian son opened our time with a prayer of thanksgiving. His mother began to speak and held back the tears. She thanked me for all we have done, for how we have changed her life and blessed her son, and how we helped their entire family. I learned that she had five sons. She thanked me for being a mother to her sons. She showed me her bank statement with her newly earned savings deposited. She told me she was an independent business owner after going through the Women's Empowerment program. It was then that I learned she had gone through the very program I was there to visit with Convoy of Hope. I had no idea that this family was blessed by two independent organizations we were supporting.

This Ethiopian mother continued to tell me that her prayers were answered as her husband just became a believer in Jesus. She told how the love of God found them all and that now they were able to see beyond their own needs to the needs of others around them. Then her son, our son, shared his words of thanks. He was thankful for the help to go to school and have meals. He was mostly thankful for the love of our family and that because of us he was able to learn about the love of Jesus. He passed a photo album I gave him with pictures of our family to his mom, and she kissed each photo and placed it next to her heart. It was a treasured gift. They then showed me a small plastic frame containing the pictures we sent them over the years. There are no words in moments like these. How can one even begin to use these instruments of language to convey the meaning of such precious encounters?

Before I knew it, my interpreter was asking me to say a few words. All that time preparing for this trip across the globe and I never once thought of what I would say when this moment arrived. I found myself once again asking God for a little help with words. With eyes wide on me, they hung on every word I said with tears of love and joy in their eyes. I shared with them how when I was a little girl and part of a family that had their own deep struggles, I was blessed by a Christian family who watched me while my parents worked. I shared how Jesus's love found me in that place through the love the Miranda family shared with me. I shared that

I came to know the love of Jesus and chose to follow Him and that my parents eventually did as well. I told them it was now a joy to bless their family just as I was once blessed. I thanked them for welcoming me into their home so warmly and for their love for me. I prayed that God would continue to bless them and keep them. And just like that, we wrapped arms around each other in a farewell embrace I will never forget. It's hard to explain all I could see in their eyes. To be there in that moment, knowing I had a part in changing this family's life forever, was so powerful. What was even more powerful was how they changed mine.

And to think, that was just the start of my trip! The rest of my time in Addis Ababa was just as powerful. This wasn't just a trip of a lifetime. It was a journey of lessons that would shape how I wanted to spend time for the rest of my life. I would go on to tour the very training center our sponsor child's mother went through to learn her trade. I would see firsthand the bright light of hope emerging in the darkness. This hope was empowering women, loving women, feeding women and their children all through a simple program. It is the work of freeing these women to fully live. It is a beautiful thing to behold.

I would visit the slum areas from where these women started—the poorest areas of the world. The raw numbers estimate one billion people on the earth live in these conditions. Most of the homes in these areas were nothing but earth floors with tree branches holding up a cloth covering for a roof. People barely dressed and barefooted were walking around, malnourished with eyes full of curiosity over our presence. A little boy was given a small candy bar and his eyes lit up. He had an oversized t-shirt on and nothing else. Slowly, he nibbled on the treat that may be his only meal that day. Another little boy came into view. A moment of beautiful generosity unfolded as the first boy, out of the little he had, chose to share it with his friend. Half a bite is better than a whole bite if it's a blessing shared between friends.

The hopelessness in the eyes of people we passed by was heartbreaking. They looked at us for answers, for help, for food, for everything they needed. The mothers with newborn infants begging for money to get milk will forever be an image that takes my breath away. Crippled people crawled on the streets to beg or look for food. They had flip flops on their hands and old tires strapped to their legs to keep them from being cut on the hot, rocky soil. Some people were crippled and disfigured to the point that, at first glance, they didn't look human at all. Those were the suffocating moments of my journey. The raw, unfiltered, and heartbreaking reality of humanity's condition East of Eden.

The injustice of it all was too much. Women bore sticks on their backs to gain a few dollars in hopes of feeding their families. All the while, this back-breaking work was slowly killing them as their internal organs were pressed beyond what they could bear. How can this even be allowed? The God I knew all these decades felt so very far away. Are we all just lost on this planet spinning out of control? Have we been abandoned and left, lost and alone? Although I had been found all those years ago, these injustices were screaming at me and I felt so very lost. I remember just crying one night into my pillow, asking so many questions to a God who seemed to be silent. I could never abandon my faith, but my faith was being challenged by all that I was experiencing.

Although I saw the impact my giving had on an Ethiopian boy and his family, there were still so many families that needed help. Although I saw the power of women blessed through a program in ways that changed the trajectory of their lives and the generations that will come after them, there was still just so much despair. These lasting impressions and pondered thoughts swirled through my soul and mind. So much had been seen through the naked eye, smelled through the nose, and felt with the embrace of arms around another soul. You have seen the images of people starving on television and the advertisements of children needing sponsorships. You know that there are billions of people going without and that you have been blessed with so much. You know it, but to see it, hear it, smell it, and walk through it—that changes you forever.

Ann Voskamp says, "It's only by amazing grace you are born where you are, to be abundant amazing grace for someone born somewhere else."[3] That's it. As I ponder all that I experienced, it became so clear to me. Once I've experienced and know the love of Jesus, I am forever found. I am then part of His rescue mission to find others in the world that need His love.

If a man has a hundred sheep and one of them wanders away, what will he do? Won't he leave the ninety-nine others on the hills and go out to search for the one that is lost? Matthew 18:12

The Good Shepherd lays His life down for the sheep and leaves the ninety-nine to go after the one that is lost. The Good Father gave His one and only son for the ninety-nine. He gave up His beloved son for the rescue of us all. He paid the ultimate price for us because we are His treasure and delight.

The Kingdom of Heaven is like a treasure that a man discovered hidden in a field. In his excitement, he hid it again and sold every-thing he owned to get enough money to buy the field. Again, the Kingdom of Heaven is like a merchant on the lookout for choice pearls. When he discovered a pearl of great value, he sold everything he owned and bought it! Matthew 13:44–46

He is our treasure. Oh beloved, you must know that you are also His treasure. He bought the field; He bought us. The pearl of great price paid the ultimate price to buy the pearls of humanity—our hearts are His treasure. There are treasures within every person on

---

[3] Voskamp, "A North American Lent."

this planet. He bought our entire field (all our dirt), so He could unearth the treasures within. He wants us to partner with Him to seek out the treasures in others. Others need us to find them and lavish His love upon them so they can know that they too have been found. Like our Creator forming us from the dirt at the dawn of time, we must be willing to get our own hands dirty to unearth the treasures of the one.

Let us determine to join Him in the ministry of reconciliation. Jesus said we would do greater works than He did. While we may not know the full revelation of what He meant, in my heart I know that we could only do greater things if we are all doing our part for His Kingdom. We just need to take seriously the role to which He calls us and be His ambassador. Those injustices we see in the world today tug at our hearts because we were created for Eden: slavery, trafficking, poverty, orphans, widows, emotionally bruised ones needing wholeness and healing. I could go on and on because the injustices are so many. They tug at our hearts because we were created for Eden. The original plan of the Father was for us to live in the garden and walk with Him in the cool of the day. We were meant for so much more than where we find ourselves today. We were never meant to experience injustice or witness the many ways it manifests around us. What I felt God speaking to me on my return trip was that I just needed to do my part. His heart is for me to join Him in loving the world to a place where they can be found. He longs for me to live in a way that brings good to others and glory to Him.

Surely your goodness and unfailing love will pursue me all the days of my life, and I will live in the house of the LORD forever. Psalm 23:6

I love how this verse speaks of His goodness and love following us all the days of our lives. It truly will follow us until we are found. Not only does it follow, chase, and pursue us all of our days, but it finds us. We allow those attributes of goodness and love to fill us by His Holy Spirit. Then His goodness and love will be left in our wake. Just as we are alive in the river of His living waters, and we have those living waters flowing in and through us, our movements through the earth should leave a wake that is noticeable to the world around us. We should have goodness, mercy, and love following behind us—a wake in our shadow that changes the world for His glory.

Beloved, be encouraged that in Christ Jesus, you are never lost but always found. Things may come at you and rattle your faith. Your feet may have to walk the dark path through the valley of the shadow of death. Deep pain and injustices may come to you, or to those you love. Through it all, His love will find you. You are never far from His presence, and I pray your soul will forever be able to sing those famous words, *"I once was lost, but now am found."* Sing these words with your life and be His hands and feet to the world in the unique way He has positioned you. If we all do our part, we will join Him in those greater works. And with His Spirit residing in us, we will have full hope that we are found in Him!

I can never escape from your Spirit! I can never get away from your presence! If I go up to heaven, you are there; if I go down to the grave, you are there. If I ride the wings of the morning, if I dwell by the farthest oceans, even there your hand will guide me, and your strength will support me. I could ask the darkness to hide me and the light around me to become night—but even in darkness I cannot hide from you. To you the night shines as bright as day. Darkness and light are the same to you. You made all the delicate, inner parts of my body and knit me together in my mother's womb. Thank you for making me so wonderfully complex! Your workmanship is marvelous—how well I know it. You watched me as I was being formed in utter seclusion, as I was woven together in the dark of the womb. You saw me before I was born. Every day of my life was recorded in your book. Every moment was laid out before a single day had passed. How precious are your thoughts about me, O God. They cannot be numbered! I can't even count them; they outnumber the grains of sand! And when I wake up, you are still with me! Psalm 139:7–18

Chapter 7

HOPE-JOYFUL PURPOSE

O n the heels of being found, our hearts can then hear the voice
of our shepherd, Jesus. We find new life in Him, for the old
is gone and all things become new. We are reclaimed and restored.
We are positioned for His amazing plans. While it may take years to
unfold, eventually the revelation of His plans come to us. Walking
in those plans, we will find ourselves walking in joyful purpose.

The months following my trip to Ethiopia were more difficult
than I thought they would be. The things I saw were at the forefront
of my mind and heart. I would cry just about every time I took a
shower, thankful beyond words that I was blessed to have running
water, as well as the countless first-world comforts that surround
me. There was almost a sense of guilt, and there were moments
when I wanted to downsize my life so I could help others in more
abundant ways. While God does actually call some people to do
just that, I knew it wasn't what He was asking of me. However, I
began to wonder what the purpose of my life really was.

Eventually, the crying in the shower lessened and life continued
on with the busyness of raising three children. I often refer to our
years in New Jersey as the "gauntlet" because our years there were
filled with some hard experiences. The years were even bookended

with my dad facing serious health issues. However, we were also very happy and enjoying where God had us in that season. The kids loved their schools. We fell in love with hosting and leading a family-friendly life group through our church. Everyone was healthy, and we had settled in New Jersey.

My husband started his own business and began working from home. This opened the door to the possibility of moving. While we had great friends in New Jersey, we were not close to our families, and there were so many areas of the country that were much cheaper—the possibilities were endless. We started having conversations about moving, dreamt of living closer to family, and started wondering if that was something God might have in store for us.

At this point, you know that John and I are not ones to make a huge life decision without praying about it. So our conversations turned into prayers, and we continued on with life as usual. I remember those days fondly, especially our Friday nights. When I picked up the older kids from school, we would start talking about what jobs everyone would do to prepare for our life group that evening. Sometimes we swung by the grocery store to pick up dessert or refreshments. Once we arrived back home, we prepared for our beloved guests' arrival. Evan was the butler: always in charge of getting the drinks ready, putting the cups out, and making sure the ice bucket was filled. Janelle would help move chairs into the living room and keep Bella entertained while I got snacks ready and printed song sheets for our time of worship together. As families arrived, Bella walked people to the coat closet. She was a genuine hostess in training. Our evenings would be filled with shared laughter, tears, fellowship, and food. We encouraged each other, worshiped together, and prayed through life's circumstances. It was a beautiful time and one of my favorite things we experienced in New Jersey.

In the summer of 2014, after a trip to see our California family and friends, God gave me a vision, which set my heart to dream.

During worship one Sunday morning, I saw myself dancing with Jesus in this beautiful field. We danced to the top of a hill and I sensed He wanted to give me a gift. My eyes were closed, and He spun me around. I came to a stop with my arms stretched out waiting to receive a gift. I felt Him say, "*Open your eyes; this is for you.*" When I did, I could see the Pacific Ocean and those all-too-familiar sea stacks off the coast. At that moment, I knew we would be moving to California. John and I still prayed and talked about the possibility of moving; however, California was not on the list of affordable states. I remember thinking that it was too much of a desire of my heart to be close to family, friends, and where we fell in love. It was my home state, and from the moment we left, I longed to return. Could it be that God was planning for us to do just that? Was this really a vision from God, with a glimpse of what was to come? Or was it my own heart's desire manifesting in my mind's eye?

I decided to tuck the vision away and trust God for clarification in His timing. At this point in my life, John and I had been married for a dozen years. All that time, my parents chose to stay together. While they mostly did their own thing, they also grew closer together. They had meals together, went on trips with friends and family together, and took on the alternating roles of caring for one another. Mom ended up with a back injury and subsequent surgery, which placed a supporting titanium cage around her spine. Dad took good care of her during her recovery. Years later, in early 2009, Dad had a stroke, which brought a conscious end to his drinking. Mom became his sole caregiver. In late August 2014, they decided to remarry, after thirty-three years of divorce. A lifelong prayer was answered, and we watched via video call as my parents remarried in a quiet ceremony in their home.

In the fall of 2014, my husband confirmed the vision God had shown me. He shared with me that after a lot of prayer, he felt that God was leading us to move back to California to enter a season of helping my parents out. Mom and Dad both had increasing health issues. And although Mom had been taking care of Dad since his stroke, his health was starting to decline. With various doctor visits on their calendar, it was getting harder for Mom to transfer Dad in and out of the wheelchair to the car. Mom's back injury had brought on chronic pain. While my parents never asked me to move back and help them, John and I knew that God was opening a door for us to be a blessing to them. And with me being an only child, there weren't siblings to help share the load.

When the ball dropped at midnight on January 1, 2015, it marked the beginning of the end of our New Jersey chapter. January would bring about a meeting with our realtor and getting things done around the house in preparation for putting it up for sale. Being an early planner and administrative type, I started calling moving companies to get quotes. Once a company was selected, I requested the first delivery of moving boxes so I could get to packing. Our hope was that our kids could finish the school year and we would see the sale of our home with a closing date that would meet the school year's end perfectly.

A busy season of raising our kids ended up being all the busier with packing, open houses, and having to leave so our home could be shown to potential buyers. Meanwhile, my dad's health was declining. He was in and out of hospitals and rehab facilities. He was getting weak, and it seemed he was losing the will to live. Doctors were dumbfounded and we had no clue as to what was causing this decline. I was unsure if I needed to jump on a plane and fly home to say goodbye in person. On three different occasions, I said goodbye to him over the phone because we weren't sure if he was going to make it. It was a difficult time.

My mind was concerned about my dad, yet I also had to focus on packing and being a momma. I would drop the older kids off at school and return home to get as much done as I could. Bella would play at my side, keeping herself busy with a handful of toys we left out of the boxes. On one occasion, she got a hold of my thick black marker for labeling boxes and proceeded to draw all over herself. Thankfully, there was a pack of baby wipes nearby, and as soon as I saw her, I grabbed them and started wiping her skin. To my surprise, the wipes actually got all of the markers off of her. Bella is not only our miracle baby, she also has more energy than our other two children combined. Keeping up with her was a full-time job, so when her nap time came around, I would try to rest.

Those rest times became pondering moments for me. I started reflecting on our time in New Jersey and how God had blessed us. I led a life group for stay-at-home moms and their kids where I led worship and had the chance to encourage moms and pray with them. It was a really sweet season. I was given the honor to speak at one of our church's Christmas Blessing Dinners, which ended up being a night of tears and laughter. As a young girl, I was so shy, you could have never convinced me to get on a stage. God saw fit to allow me to do just that, and I spoke to a room full of women. It was so encouraging to hear many women come to me afterward for weeks on end, thanking me for the ways God spoke through me to their heart. I also began training for the prayer ministry team. My love for prayer grew in huge ways, and it started to feel like a calling. John and I saw a season of extravagant giving where we were supporting a variety of ministries and causes that were making eternal impacts for the Glory of God and the good of humanity. We were pouring into the lives of families through our Friday night small group and making lifelong friends in the process. My heart became full of thanks for all the ways we were pouring into others. This other-focused way of life had in a way brought us to life. And it brought us much joy.

I had always loved and believed the promise that God had a plan for my life. Most people will often quote verse 11 from the passage below. Yet as I was reading the entire chapter one day, this section stood out to me. While I wouldn't say my thirteen years of living on the East Coast was a season of captivity or loss of fortune, the transition of returning to my native land of California made this feel like a full-circle moment. God had indeed sent me to other states and now He was bringing me home.

"For I know the plans I have for you," says the Lord. "They are plans for good and not for disaster, to give you a future and a hope. In those days when you pray, I will listen. If you look for me wholeheartedly, you will find me. I will be found by you," says the Lord. "I will end your captivity and restore your fortunes. I will gather you out of the nations where I sent you and will bring you home again to your own land."
Jeremiah 29:11–14

The things I faced in New Jersey caused me to face God more than ever before. I was praying more, reading the Word of God more, and seeking Him all the more. His voice became louder than all the others, and He was revealing encouraging truths to me. I found myself writing more and more and then sharing what I wrote with my small group of friends. The more I shared, the more others were encouraged and the more I started to see the plans God had for me.

God has a joyful purpose for me to encourage others, pray, write, and live a life of loving others by giving generously of my time, talent, and treasure. I knew that whatever the next season held, I was called to walk out His joyful purpose for me. It reminded me of an acronym for JOY I had heard as a young child—Jesus, Others, You. That is a Kingdom of God perspective that will truly bring joy to our souls.

We are in a time in human history where the world tells us there is the freedom to choose who we want to be. To name our own destiny. Identify as we wish. In faith, I believe that God's Word is true and that within each person is the *imago Dei*—image of God.

So God created human beings in his own image. In the image of God
he created them; male and female he created them. Genesis 1:27

If you read the Bible or are at least vaguely familiar with the
storyline, you know that mankind falls into sin in Eden. Sin sepa-
rates us from God, just like it separated Adam and Eve from Him
and the garden. A redemption plan that was put into place before
the foundation of the earth begins to unfold. The God who created
us in His image and so loved us chose to generously give His one
and only son, Jesus, to die for our sins. Because of the death and
resurrection of Jesus, there is now a way for us to have a new life
in Christ. A metamorphosis of the spirit takes place and we are
made new. We are indeed a new creation as some translations state.
Unfurling like a majestic butterfly, we take flight to new heights
for the good of man and the glory of God.

This means that anyone who belongs to Christ has become a new
person. The old life is gone; a new life has begun! 2 Corinthians 5:17

For we are God's masterpiece. He has created us anew in Christ
Jesus, so we can do the good things he planned for us long ago.
Ephesians 2:10

Beloved, we all have a specific gift to share with the world. Each
of us was made in the image of God. If we don't share that image,
the world will never get a glimpse of that piece of the heart of God.
As you journey through your life in Christ, you will come to see His
joyful purpose for you. It was in New Jersey that I began to realize
God had filled me with faith, powerful prayers, generosity of heart,
and encouraging words.

Eventually, God allowed the sale of our home to have a closing
date that indeed lined up with the end of the school year. While
we didn't yet have a home waiting for us in California, we could

count on my parents for a place to stay. As springtime came to a close, we found ourselves closing our New Jersey chapter with farewell gatherings that were so bittersweet. Our life group saw its final gathering, and we were surrounded with love and hugs from friends we will cherish for eternity. Our church had a going-away party for us and surrounded us with beautiful prayers and blessings. Our hearts would miss these beloved friends more than words could say, but we were thankful for each and every one of them. We were thankful for the many lessons we learned in the gauntlet, and we were excited about the new frontier before us.

A new frontier—it was one of the phrases God put on my heart for this new season. Like many families of the Oregon Trail days of old, we were heading West. Our journey may have looked a lot different. The majority of our belongings were packed up and being stored until we could get to California and find a home to place them in. Our select few items came along with us for the cross-country trek. The older kids finished their last day of sixth and second grade and we piled into the car to start our westward journey with a few planned stops along the way.

We went from New Jersey to Virginia to visit grandparents, aunties, uncles, and cousins. Sweet summer moments on the river with loved ones made for a great start to our trip. In total, we took about fifteen days to get to California. We enjoyed stops visiting family and friends across the country. One of our favorite stops was in Hannibal, Missouri, Mom's hometown. We stayed with my auntie and uncle. They gave us a tour of the town, which included seeing the house where Mom grew up, the very one the grandfather I never met built with his own hands. We saw the restaurant they owned, where Mom worked alongside my grandmother as they navigated life after grandfather's all-too-early passing. Our kids especially enjoyed touring through the Mark Twain Caves! These were literally the old stomping grounds of Mom and her sisters. It was a place of history, nestled near the grand Mississippi River, in the heart of our country. Those moments in Missouri now hold a special spot in my heart.

As we continued on, visiting John's older brother and family in Nebraska, we saw old covered wagons along Interstate 80. There are literally ruts in the ground today left from those wagon trains of the past. The journey of others that began around 1811 made an impression in the soil that has remained to this day. There is something about seeing those remains that make you feel so small in the grand story of humanity, and yet give you a longing to be part of a story that is greater than yourself. I was beginning to realize that our lives leave a trail and mark the ground of the lives around us. Those markings can be positive or negative. How we live our lives will impact others. Oh, that we would leave a trail of Kingdom, glory-changing lives with God's love for the better.

We all have the power to touch another's life. Just our passing through from one location to another has the power to make an impression with lasting effects. It's actually what we were made for. The God of the universe longs for us to join the beautiful story He is writing of us. It's an epic story of love and joy.

Fixing our eyes on Jesus, the pioneer and perfecter of faith. For the joy set before him he endured the cross, scorning its shame, and sat down at the right hand of the throne of God. Hebrews 12:2 NIV

For the Kingdom of God is not a matter of what we eat or drink, but of living a life of goodness and peace and joy in the Holy Spirit. Romans 14:17

Do you not know, beloved, that you are the joy set before Him? Jesus faced the cross in obedience to the Father's will, but you were the joy of why He chose to endure the cross. Now you are His and He is yours and His banner over you will always and forever be love—not condemnation, shame, or ridicule, only the never-ending love of God. He longs for you to remain in His love for you, to have His joy overflowing, and to leave eternal impressions by producing lasting fruit with the vapor of your life.

I have loved you even as the Father has loved me. Remain in my love. When you obey my commandments, you remain in my love, just as I obey my Father's commandments and remain in his love. I have told you these things so that you will be filled with my joy. Yes, your joy will overflow! This is my commandment: Love each other in the same way I have loved you. There is no greater love than to lay down one's life for one's friends. You are my friends if you do what I command. I no longer call you slaves, because a master doesn't confide in his slaves. Now you are my friends, since I have told you everything the Father told me. You didn't choose me. I chose you. I appointed you to go and produce lasting fruit, so that the Father will give you whatever you ask for, using my name. This is my command: Love each other.
John 15:9–17

There is a role that only you can play in God's epic love story. There are specific things you were created to do. When you step into that role, you will find true life. The abundant life Jesus died to give you. Whatever He calls you to, do it with all that you are for His glory.

So whether you eat or drink, or whatever you do, do it all for the glory of God. 1 Corinthians 10:31

I knew that our move to California would provide a whole new chapter of opportunities for our family to walk in that joyful purpose. We knew it was time to be near my parents so we could help them out. We were willing to move across the country to do just that, and we would purpose to do it for the glory of God. Our exciting adventure across the country was bittersweet for me. Not only was it difficult to leave behind many cherished friendships, but the entire time we were traveling my dad was getting weaker. He was fresh out of another hospital stay and recovering in a skilled nursing facility. Every day I would check in with a phone call to Mom, letting her know of our cross-country progress and asking how Dad was doing. The element of the unknown had me wondering if at some point during our travel, I would need John to drop me off at the nearest airport so I could fly to California. Thankfully, we didn't have to do that.

On July 2, 2015, we arrived in California, safe and sound. The many prayers of family and friends for traveling mercies were answered. After a stretch of the legs and lots of hugs from Mom, we spent some time resting. We were able to stop by in the afternoon and visit Dad at his skilled nursing facility, where we learned he would be released to go home the next day. I was thankful beyond words that God heard my prayers and Dad was still with us. The doctors put in orders for him to have a nurse from the home health program come out and check on him a couple of times a week. After our visit with Dad, we headed home to settle in at my parents' house. We didn't have a home of our own yet and planned on staying with them until we found one.

As it turned out, that vision God gave me of the coast of California, and the thoughts I had, came true. God brought me full circle. We didn't have a home, a school for the kids, or our household things, but we had family and a trust that God would give us all we needed for the new frontier ahead. We were filled with excitement and a long to-do list. Dad was able to come home the day after we arrived, and we spent that first weekend, Independence Day weekend, enjoying being on solid ground. Don't get me wrong, I love a good road trip, and the one we experienced was epic indeed. However, it felt so good to just be still and rest, knowing we were right where God wanted us to be.

It was a good weekend—then Monday arrived. Mondays tend to be my least favorite day of the week. Fresh starts are great, but sometimes you don't want the refreshment of the weekend to end. However, this Monday I was able to help my parents by taking Dad to a follow-up doctor visit with his primary care physician. Despite an initial high blood pressure reading due to a bit of white coat syndrome, Dad's pressure came into a normal range and the doctor told us he looked good. We were advised to follow up in two months. When we arrived back home, Dad was struggling a bit to get in the door. We got him into a wheelchair and rolled him into the living room. It was then that he had a massive seizure in front of my son, my husband, and me. We called 911, and while we waited for them to arrive, my thoughts started swirling. Did we come all this way for my dad to die right before us? How would my kids be affected by the unknown of what we would face in this new chapter? Will we see Dad again? Was he even able to hear me telling him it would be okay? The paramedics came, and in a few blinks, they had Dad on the stretcher. The ambulance doors shut. John, Evan, and I just stood there hugging each other.

At that moment, I wasn't sure if I had it in me to handle what this new frontier had in store. I needed a strength that would carry me through the great unknowns ahead. I wondered how I would be able to continue on in God's joyful purposes for me when there was such a heartbreaking moment facing me. We must allow His Spirit to empower us. Then and only then can we fully join Him in His plans for us. He will give us all we need for this life.

I pray that from his glorious, unlimited resources he will empower you with inner strength through his Spirit. Ephesians 3:16

I asked the Holy Spirit to empower me for what was to come, because in and of myself, I felt powerless. Mom and I grabbed a few things and headed to the hospital. We would eventually find out through a simple ultrasound test the reason for Dad's continued decline. His right carotid artery was 100 percent blocked and his left carotid artery was over 90 percent blocked. Dad would need to be transferred to a hospital across town for life-saving surgery to have a stent placed in the left artery. We prayed with him in the ER before they transported him to the other hospital. Honestly, I don't think we stopped praying through the entire ordeal.

Dad's surgery was a success, and he had to spend some time in the ICU recovering, along with another stay at a skilled nursing facility. God saved his life, and we were so thankful our prayers had been answered. When I saw him the night of the surgery in the ICU, he was awake and joking with us like his usual self. His personality, will to live, and desire to eat had all returned. What could have been a tragedy turned into a miracle. I know that it was only by the power of the Spirit of God residing in me that I had the strength to make it through this ordeal without breaking down. It was only by the Spirit of God that I was sheltered from the trauma of the moments we faced. And it's only by His Spirit that I would be able to withstand the many similar moments that would continue to unfold in our new frontier.

God is our shelter and strength, always ready to help in times of trouble. Psalm 46:1 Good News Translation

Beloved, as you obediently walk in His joyful purposes for you, you will need His Spirit to strengthen you. Traumatic situations will likely unfold. Heartbreaking scenarios are a very real possibility. He has promised to be with you through it all. He is faithful to be your everything. You were not created for independence, so depend on His Spirit for all you need, and walk confidently into His joyful purpose.

Chapter 8

HOPE-HEALING
FORGIVENESS

S tepping into a new frontier can be messy. Settling into a new
frontier takes time, and it's guaranteed to be uncharted territory. One never really knows how to prepare for the new. Often,
we are thrust into the new and we just have to start running. When
we moved to our new frontier of California, I knew it would usher
us into a new season. God placed it on our hearts to be there for
my parents, so I knew that this season would bring about opportunities to help them. It also brought newness as we settled into a
new church, found a school for the kids, and after a few weeks, a
home of our own.

One of the things I have come to enjoy about moving over the
years is the fresh start and clean-slate feeling. On August 20, 2015,
the movers arrived with our belongings, and we began to settle into
the beautiful new home God provided for us. We actually signed
the papers and received the keys to our home three weeks before our
belongings arrived. However, it didn't stop us from spending those
last few weeks of the summer swimming in our new pool. Bella

called our new house the big splash and fell in love with the palm trees at first sight. I was so touched that God led us to a home that had such a retreat-like setting for our family to enjoy, and it was topped off with a handful of redwood trees, which have always been a favorite of mine. The way they grow together in family circles is beautiful. The majesty displayed in the way they stand tall and point to the heavens has always had a way of pointing my heart to the Creator God. These marvels of creation grow hundreds of feet into the sky and yet have roots that are only six to ten feet deep. It's the intertwining of their root system that gives them their unique strength. You could say they are better together, and they are a picture of what a family looks like. Every place we have lived, God has tucked in some little surprise that makes my heart happy—and those trees were one of them for me.

Another surprise was an in-law setup on the main floor. We knew the moment we saw this home that this space would be something we could possibly use in the future for my parents. As we settled in, John used the spare bedroom as office space for his business. The extra kitchen counter area became a well-used space for the kids to work on school projects. I set up an office area of my own in the in-law living room space with dreams of writing this very book you are reading. I knew this season would bring me to the moments of writing this book, I just didn't know how long it would take to actually find those moments.

Unpacking and settling into our new home was mixed with preparing the older kids for a new school year. Six days after we moved our belongings into our home, the school year started. Nerves were running high as Bella and I dropped off her siblings to start their first day of seventh and third grade. Once they were off and my nerves calmed a bit, Bella and I were off and running—running right into the unknown of this new frontier. I started realizing quickly that when your season is one of uncharted territory, you will run into the bumps of the road, fall into a few ditches, and even hit some walls as you explore the unknown, charting the land with your everyday life. The kids seemed to be settling in and were kept busy with school assignments and jumping into the pool for "one last swim, Mommy, please!" Working from home was working well for John. I was finding new ways to keep Bella entertained at the various doctor visits for my parents that filled my days.

Dad's health stabilized after his life-saving surgery. Eventually, he settled back at home with Mom caring for him twenty-four seven. Not only did he survive the massive stroke in 2009, but God gave him another lease on life through that surgery. We were thankful to be living close to family. For the first time, we were able to host my parents for Thanksgiving dinner. For the first time, we were able to attend church with Mom on a weekly basis. For the first time, I stepped into a women's ministry role leading a monthly event called IF:Table and an annual event called IF:Local through IF:Gathering—events that Mom and lifelong friends were able to attend with me. Family dinners at Mom and Dad's house were happening, and I got to see them beaming with joy enjoying frequent visits from their grandchildren. We were able to attend barbecues and holiday dinners with California cousins, aunts, uncles, and many friends we hadn't seen for thirteen years! There were a lot of firsts, and we were thankful for all of them.

We were settling in nicely, albeit at a faster rate than I thought was possible. The feeling of being thrust into the new frontier was very real. Mom and Dad had various doctor visits for their various health conditions. It was getting harder and harder for Bella to sit still through these boring times. Thankfully, there were some friends who offered to hang out with her, which made her day and was like a refreshing drink of water for me. Evan was making buddies at school and enjoyed having a good friend next door. Janelle was quieter and this girl who loved to sing at the top of her lungs growing up seemed to lose her song. I couldn't remember the last time I saw her open her mouth and sing on a Sunday during worship, or in the car when a favorite song came on. It is hard to move across the country and leave good friends behind. It's even harder to be thrust into a season where your grandparents are facing so many health challenges. While we were very thankful for the many firsts of this new frontier, there were things from the old territory that we all missed terribly. Janelle has always been a sweet girl and has kept an open communication with her father and me—a gift that we treasure as her parents. Our desire is to parent first, but we are thankful that our kids are friends with us second! There were moments where tears were shed over missed friendships and the difficulty of finding her place in a school filled with kids who knew each other since kindergarten.

Part of me longed to just go away for a few days on a girls' weekend and have deep talks, good laughs, and snotty cries with my firstborn. The season we were in just didn't allow for it, and I felt the pull of helping my parents pulling me away from my own children more often than I would have liked. I became all the more thankful for a loving husband who was also able to work from home, which gave him the flexibility to watch the kids at times that I was needed at a parent's side. Mom had a couple of foot surgeries, and both her and Dad ended up visiting the hospital more and more frequently. Janelle seemed to get all the quieter, and my heart started to just hurt in ways it hadn't in years. I kept telling myself that Janelle just needed time to adjust and make new friends and the teen years were just around the corner. I knew that as a firstborn, she was the type of kid to shoulder more than she needed to. She felt, in a way, that if she kept her own struggles to herself it was a way of helping me in a season that was so demanding. In giving her time, I would from time-to-time ask her if there was anything she wanted to discuss. While the usual drama of junior high would come up in late-night talks now and then, she mostly told me that everything was fine. The look in her eyes and the loss of her song told my momma heart otherwise. So I prayed that God would meet her right where she was. That whatever was bothering her would not be something serious and that if she needed to talk to me, she would do just that. I prayed and I prayed.

Before I knew it, a year and a half flew by. Mom made it through another surgery, and Dad seemed to be visiting the hospital more and more. Janelle was feeling sick here and there with an upset stomach, which was anxiety and depression manifesting itself in her body. I started feeling that all of this was my fault. I still didn't know what was going on, but I did what mommas at times do and blamed myself. If I hadn't moved her across the country and away from her good friends, this wouldn't be happening. If I hadn't brought her to a place where she had to witness her grandparents' health declining in some very scary situations, this wouldn't be happening. If, if, if. All the while, I was ministering through a ministry by the same name, IF. IF:Gathering is a wonderful ministry to women. They provide discipleship tools to equip women in the local church to know God in real ways.

IF:Gathering exists to equip women with gospel-centered resources, events, and community so that they may learn about who God is and disciple other women right where they are.[4]

I attended an IF:Local annual event on a February weekend in New Jersey in 2015. A friendly mom at the kid's school invited me, and although I didn't know anyone at the event besides her, I felt drawn to be there. The first night as I walked through the threshold of the front door, I felt God speak to my heart. *"My Beloved, when you get to California, you will be leading an IF:Local."* My answer to Him in the moment was of course a "Yes." However, I didn't even know what He was signing me up for. Couldn't I get a glimpse of this ministry before He called me to it? It seems his usual protocol is to call us when we don't feel equipped and have no real clue what He is truly calling us to do.

---

[4] IF:Gathering, "Our Vision."

One look at the many stories of the Old Testament will show you exactly what I mean. Abraham was called to leave his family and go to a land that God would show him. He had to obey and walk in faith, following the direction of God as He went. There was no map and no clear picture as to why he was being asked to go. Four hundred years later, his descendant Moses was told to take the Israelites out of slavery and into a promised land. What he didn't know is that it would be a forty-year journey with a bunch of grumbling people and the people would enter the promised land without him. Time and time again throughout the Bible, simple people of faith were called to what would seem like impossible missions. Some saw the promises of God fulfilled and some simply lived in obedience only for the promise to be fulfilled through future generations. All of them lived in faith according to the promise and walked in obedience to the call.

That night, I said "yes" to God before I knew what I was getting into, and by the end of the weekend, I fell in love with a movement of women who were set out to make disciples who, then, make disciples. It was a beautiful weekend of unity and simplicity of the Good News. God was made real in ways that were making women come alive with hearts for others to know Him as they did. We received amazing insights, encouragement, and teaching through some simple yet amazing women of faith. And we were given time to respond to how God spoke to us throughout our time together. This IF:Gathering movement was just what I needed and something I was excited to bring with me to my new frontier. God was showing me that there would be many "what if?" moments in life. The greatest "if" about which we needed to be concerned was an early phrase at the gathering: "*If God is real, we want more than anything to live like it.*"[5] YES! My heart said YES!

---

[5] Allen, IF:Gathering 2015.

So I followed through on that yes and began pouring into women. While I was seeing women uniting across denominational lines, growing in their faith and friendships with each other, the many "what ifs" of my own season were screaming at me. What if we lose one of my parents? What if the kids don't make good friends? What if Janelle never gets her joy and her song back? What if I am not strong enough for this season? I was determined to continue on in this new frontier and trust God with the many "what ifs."

On a beautiful May evening, my husband and I were visiting with a good friend. We were having good, deep-faith conversations, which are my favorite kind. We were sharing our heart with her about how we just didn't know what was going on with Janelle and how we longed for God to show us. This season seemed to be drowning out our chance to have an honest conversation with our own daughter. We closed our time together in prayer, and our friend saw a picture in her spirit. She shared it with us and said, "There is something you need to look at in Janelle's room on her desk." The next day, our first-born daughter would be gone for the day celebrating her eighth-grade graduation with her class at an amusement park. As soon as I got home from dropping Evan off at school, I went straight to Janelle's room. A journal, a website, and some sketches unfolded a story that had me asking more questions. While the details of what we found are her story to tell, we knew that our sweet girl was facing anxiety and depression on a level that needed intervention. There were dark things she needed to face, and we were there that evening to face them with her. Things that were pulling her into dark places of seclusion needed to be brought into the light.

We prayed with her and had a deep and hard conversation. Our girl who had not shown much in the way of emotion other than anger for a while broke before our eyes. The love we covered her with and the way we showed care for what she was facing allowed her tears to flow. She found herself in a place where she believed the lie that God was not listening to her. However, that night she also found the truth that indeed he heard and answered her deepest cry. She prayed that the darkness she was in would be brought to the light and that we would find out, so she didn't have to come to us with it. It's hard to admit that you are depressed and anxious, and the enemy of our souls wants to make sure no one ever finds out when we are feeling that way. His desire is to isolate us in our pain. Thankfully, God intervened and prompted us to take a deeper look at things that were on the surface and in plain sight, all through the vision a friend shared with us. God heard Janelle's cry for help after all. That night she talked to us about how she was feeling, what she was going through, and she felt our great love for her the whole way through.

Janelle graduated from eighth grade a few days after God answered her cry for help. Her journey to healing began with an entrance into the first month of summer vacation where she had no phone, tablet, laptop, or internet access. There were things that pulled her in ways that were unhealthy, and as much as she hated it, for her healing we had to lay down some hard lines. I am not telling others how to parent, but there are times when love has to be tough in putting boundaries in place. It's a very loving thing to remove something that is harming your child so they can begin to heal. These things can become addictions, and they have real consequences and effects on our beloved, innocent children. We must do what we can to aid in their healing. No teenager on the verge of entering high school wants to start a summer with those kinds of restrictions. It wasn't easy, but Janelle began to heal. Eventually, she even began to sing again. Then the next shoe dropped.

A summer of intense hospital moments for Dad ensued. His strength was weakening, and after a few falls, it was evident that he would not be able to live at home with Mom anymore. We had to quickly find a place that could care for him. Thankfully, a social worker was able to lead us to a board-and-care home that would fit in my parents' very tight budget. The summer of 2017 was one of intense activity. Moving my dad into his new home, which was about thirty minutes from where we lived, and setting up some new doctors for him were priorities. I also started to look into ways that could possibly get my dad some assistance through veteran's programs and local agencies. Dad was stable in his new home, and Mom was facing an empty home and the sadness this change brought with their separation.

Summer came to an end as school began. Janelle had begun the journey of healing from anxiety and depression, and entered ninth grade. Evan was starting his last year of elementary school, and Bella would be our first child to attend pre-K. This season just wouldn't allow me the time with Bella that she needed to prepare for kindergarten at home as I had with Janelle and Evan. While Bella only went three days a week, and a half of a day at that, it was a treasured time for her to play and learn with buddies. As October rolled around, we heard that there would be no aid options for my dad through the programs available. It quickly became evident that in order to afford to pay for his care, my parents would have to sell the only family home I had known growing up. In a matter of three months, I helped my mom go through forty years of belongings and downsize to the in-law setup of our home. My husband found office space to rent, and our weekends were spent moving him into that space so we could open up space for Mom to move in with us.

While this flurry of activity was going on, Janelle opened up to us in sharing another painful piece of her story that she was too afraid to share with us during our early summer conversation. Janelle was also navigating a wounding from church that once again is her story to tell. My own church-wounded heart was hurting all over again as I watched her face this pain. The wound affected all of us and had its way of opening up the wound I experienced in the past. By the end of 2017, Mom moved into our home, Evan started not feeling well, and it became evident that in order for our sweet Janelle Hope to heal further, we had to find a new church in this new frontier. On the last day of the year, God, in His wondrous ways, led us to that new church, which just happened to be called New Hope. The hope we had in Jesus didn't need to change; however, we needed it to become new and fresh to our wounded and hurting family. We needed our sweet girl to be made new.

New Hope Church had signs out front that said, "Welcome Home." God had us enter a season in our new frontier where our home and family would be the focus, as He allowed healing to begin in our hearts. As we navigated a new church, Janelle's healing, and adjusting to Mom moving in with us, it felt as if my wounds of the past came rushing to the surface. They were hitting me fast and hard as I adjusted to living with my mom after all these years. As a young girl, there were many things I faced that at the moment had to be pushed under the surface. I had never been to counseling, and the traumatic emotion of the past was crashing over me. It didn't help that my son started to have gastrointestinal issues that were becoming more worrisome. It didn't help that my firstborn was navigating the healing of a church wound. It didn't help that I had my own various church wounds opening up all over again. I kept feeling like I just needed some space to breathe and scream, and I was desperate for a counselor to help me navigate all of the emotions.

If we don't allow God to heal our emotional wounds, then we run the risk of leading our lives from a wounded place. God's own Son, Jesus, not only died to save us from sin, but He took upon His flesh the stripes that bring our healing.

But He was wounded for our transgressions, He was bruised for our iniquities; the chastisement for our peace was upon Him, and by His stripes we are healed. Isaiah 53:5 NKJV

It became vital that I allow Jesus, the Good Shepherd, to heal my wounds. I needed to allow His love and grace to flow from me to others. I needed His forgiveness to freely flow through me and keep my heart far from offenses and bitterness. He freely forgave me, and I needed to freely forgive all over again. I had known for a long time that His perfect love in me was the only way I was able to forgive at all.

Hatred stirs up strife, but love covers all offenses. Proverbs 10:12 ESV

John 8:1–11 tells the story of a woman caught in adultery. The religious leaders of the day brought the woman in front of a crowd to whom Jesus was speaking. These leaders reminded Jesus that the law of Moses stated she should be stoned for her actions. Then they asked Jesus what He would do. They were demanding an answer—demanding justice. Don't we feel the same when hurt is inflicted upon us? We long for justice, and we want the person who hurt us to pay for what they did. Now we may not go as far as desiring to stone them, but we want justice. The crowd in this story didn't let up, and Jesus finally responded.

They kept demanding an answer, so he stood up again and said, "All right, but let the one who has never sinned throw the first stone!" John 8:7

One by one the accusers slipped away until only the woman and Jesus remained. Jesus was the only person in the crowd that day who was without sin. He was the only one who could fulfill the directive He gave to the religious leaders. However, He chose grace and mercy. He didn't condemn or accuse her but encouraged her to leave and stop sinning. Jesus extended healing forgiveness. When He died on the cross, He paid the price for all of our sins. So, beloved, when someone sins against you and that feeling of a need for justice, revenge, or someone to pay comes over you, remember— Jesus paid the price. He was sinless yet chose to take on the sins of the world so that we could be forgiven and also forgive others. As far as casting a stone, the morning of the resurrection, Jesus cast one stone for all mankind. It was the stone that rolled away. Oh, that we would follow in His kind and gentle footsteps.

Instead, be kind to each other, tenderhearted, forgiving one another, just as God through Christ has forgiven you. Ephesians 4:32

I found myself in uncharted territory, needing His hope to be new and fresh, and needing His love to cover all those offenses. As only He can do, God brought me to a place where He could do just that. In 2018, we faced an intense summer. I have a reminder of it in my Bible to this day, which states, "Nine weeks, five people, thirty-four doctor visits." My parents had their health situations, and our son was navigating one of his own. We were trying to find answers as to why he kept having severe abdominal pain and sickness. In the middle of summer, a friend asked me to an event at a local church. Honestly, it was the last thing I wanted to be doing in the middle of all I was facing. However, I felt God tugging at my heart to go, and so I gave Him my "yes" yet again. I picked up my friend and we headed to hear an out-of-town speaker share her testimony. When the evening concluded, there was a time for prayer ministry. While my friend sat in her chair, I couldn't get to the altar fast enough. I was desperate for a touch from the Good Shepherd. I needed to hear His voice. I needed a miracle to wash away the flooding emotions and many wounds of the past.

At the altar, a woman who I didn't know prayed over me. I didn't tell her what I needed—she just started praying over me. This woman of faith told me, "I feel like the Father wants me to sing a father's blessing over you." She proceeded to sing a prayer blessing into my ear as she hugged me, and it was as if the Father came down from heaven to embrace my wounded heart. The emotional floodwaters started to rise, and the woman then said, "Is it okay if I give you a mother's blessing?" I just nodded my head, not aware of just how special this blessing would be. Before she prayed a blessing over me, she said that she felt God wanted her to speak to me in the place of a mother. She started out by apologizing for being a mother who put me to the side as if I had been tossed in a box. She asked me to forgive her for not being what I needed when I was little, for not seeing me and loving me better. The healing waters began to flow in the form of tears and forgiveness given. Her blessing was like a healing oil straight from heaven. That evening, God allowed His Holy Spirit to minister healing through a woman I had never met. She prayed with me against the trauma of the past and all those old wounds. That night, I met the Comforter that Jesus prayed for in a new way. The Helper He sent after ascending to the Father in heaven. The Holy Spirit did in one night what earthly counseling takes years to do. Healing oil covered every wounded place within me.

And I will pray the Father, and he shall give you another Comforter, that he may abide with you for ever. John 14:16 KJV

In Psalm 23 NIV, there is a portion of verse 5 that states, *"You anoint my head with oil."*

Jesus is our Good Shepherd and His oil brings healing and protection. Shepherds used oil as protection from biting insects. If left untreated, a wound from a biting insect would cause the sheep intense pain. The sheep, in an effort to ease the pain, would ram its head into a rock, potentially fracturing its own skull and causing death. Shepherds would also use oil on open wounds to aid in healing their sheep. You see, beloved, no word of apology from man will heal you like the oil of your Good Shepherd. We must first bring our wounds to Him for the healing that we seek. Once His oil is freely poured out, it can also be a protection for us. We cannot allow ourselves to walk around like a bitten sheep, beating our heads into the ground. Replaying a hurt and allowing the offenses of others to repeat in our heads can cause bitterness and unforgiveness to kill us.

We must trust Jesus in the process of our healing. He is the wounded healer, and we too can be used by Him in bringing healing to others. He knows the depth of our pain like no other. Between the garden and Sunday morning, Jesus took upon Himself not only the sin of all mankind but their sorrows as well. These sorrows are the effects of sin and the depths of despair mankind faces because of sin. He took it all. He experienced it all before we were knit together in our mother's womb. He took the burden of sorrows so that our yoke would be easy and our burden would be light. I believe the enemy intended for the pain we experience to feel deeper than what we actually feel. We experience a lighter, easier pain because Jesus took the brunt of it on our behalf!

He was despised and rejected—a man of sorrows, acquainted with deepest grief. We turned our backs on him and looked the other way. He was despised, and we did not care. Isaiah 53:3

For my yoke is easy to bear, and the burden I give you is light. Matthew 11:30

On the heels of this highlight of my summer night of healing moment, God highlighted the story of Hagar to me. If we go all the way back to the beginning of the Bible, we see Hagar who is with child, running from Sarai. Abram and Sarai were promised descendants that would outnumber the stars; however, Sarai was barren. While clinging to this promise, they wondered if instead of waiting they should do something. Sarai gave her maidservant, Hagar, to Abram in hopes that she would conceive. Hagar does just that and Sarai begins to treat her harshly. Eventually, Hagar runs out of town. Hurt by what we could easily call the church of the day, Hagar finds herself alone in the wilderness. Let's pause and step back in time to see how the story plays out.

The angel of the LORD found Hagar beside a spring of water in the wilderness, along the road to Shur. The angel said to her, "Hagar, Sarai's servant, where have you come from, and where are you going?"

"I'm running away from my mistress, Sarai," she replied.

The angel of the LORD said to her, "Return to your mistress, and submit to her authority." Then he added, "I will give you more descendants than you can count."

And the angel also said, "You are now pregnant and will give birth to a son. You are to name him Ishmael (which means 'God hears'), for the LORD has heard your cry of distress. This son of yours will be a wild man, as untamed as a wild donkey! He will raise his fist against everyone, and everyone will be against him. Yes, he will live in open hostility against all his relatives."

Thereafter, Hagar used another name to refer to the LORD, who had spoken to her. She said, "You are the God who sees me." She also said, "Have I truly seen the One who sees me?" Genesis 16:7–13

Isn't this a beautiful picture of how God sees our hurts, even if they are inflicted by His chosen people, the church? I have heard it said that there are no perfect churches, but there are healthy churches. This story of Hagar is one of being hurt, but also by being seen by God in that hurt. The one who felt shunned by God's chosen people was chosen by God to bear a son with a name that would forever remind her that God heard her cry. This wounded woman of faith would become the first woman to give God a specific name and henceforth would refer to Him as El Roi, Hebrew for "The God who sees me."

With my own wounds healed in such a powerful way, I was seeing my daughter's wounds with more clarity. I was able to walk through her healing with clear eyes. He was showing me that before she even felt wounded by the church, she had her own Hagar moment of knowing Him as the God who saw her. That night when we had our hard conversation and her cry had been heard, He revealed the truth that He saw her in her deep pain. When we are struggling in the depths of pain, we often cannot see God. It's in those times that we all need the Holy Spirit to remind us of a very important truth. While we may not see Him, God sees us. A good friend of mine had her own realization of this truth and put it into her own words. Referring to God, Tara Cho said, "You were just waiting to be called into the struggle."

The Good Shepherd didn't just heal my wounds, He was also healing our family's wounds. When we allow His oil to heal us, His voice begins to drown out all the others. All those words that cause wounds to fade and the Word's (Jesus's) wounds bring healing. Beloved, there are wounds in the literal Body of Christ so Jesus alone can step into the wounds of the Body of Christ, the church, to bring healing. As the church, we are called to fill the great commission: to make disciples of all nations and to be known by our love for one another. As God continued to bring new hope and healing, my deep prayer for the church all the more became that we would be united in Him—that we would no longer be a bride that is self-inflicting wounds but accepting each other in love. Jesus will be returning for a spotless bride, and we need to allow His oil to bring about healing.

The call on Jesus's life was to bring healing forgiveness to the world. When His healing touches our deepest wounds, His forgiveness can then freely flow from our hearts toward others. As we allow Him to bring this kind of wholeness to our lives, His oil anoints us and a heart of healing forgiveness both positions us and protects, allowing us to forgive as He did. Only then can we echo the prayer He prayed from His cross as we bear our own.

Father, forgive them, for they don't know what they are doing.
Luke 23:34

You see, beloved, when we, as the church, inflict a wound on a fellow believer, we are inflicting a wound on the very body of Christ. If we only knew what we were doing, we would stop and let love cover it all. When others bring an offense toward us, we take the higher ground. This means kneeling at the foot of the cross on the hill called Calvary. Choosing to bring every hurt and offense to the base of that cross where His blood spilled and soaked into the earth He created. Allowing His love to cover a multitude of sins and offenses. Choosing to cast grace to those who offend us instead of casting stones of unforgiving judgment.

I truly believe that allowing the Holy Spirit to cultivate a healing forgiveness in you can be a means of protection. When we are quick to forgive and extend grace to those who have wronged us, it covers us so that the roots of bitterness cannot take to the soil of our soul. We must also remember that while forgiveness can be extended, it isn't always received. Sometimes we forgive people after they have died or with whom we are no longer in touch. However, do not allow the enemy to tell you the lie that in order for true forgiveness to happen a relationship must be restored. Jesus died, past tense, for the forgiveness of mankind's sins. It is a gift freely offered to us. Our relationship with Jesus is only restored when we show true repentance for our actions and accept His forgiveness. There will be times when relationships are not restored, and this is a pain that Jesus knows all too well. I am not advocating toxic relationships in which a victim continues to forgive and is walked on over and over again. We must have healthy boundaries in place—healthy fences without allowing the offenses to keep us from healing forgiveness.

Beloved, no matter what sorrows you face, remember that God sees you. He has a record of every tear you cry. He experienced it in the garden of Gethsemane and on the cross of Calvary. He is intimately aware of the depth of your sorrows and grief.

You keep track of all my sorrows. You have collected all my tears in your bottle. You have recorded each one in your book. Psalm 56:8

Yes, this new frontier was one for the record books. Yes, there were almost constant changes and many unknowns around every corner. A third of our 2018 summer was filled with doctor visits. Yes, we were still trying to figure out what was happening in our son's body. Yes, my childhood emotional traumatic wounds were lavished in healing oil in what I still refer to as a miracle. Yes, we were falling more in love with our New Hope family and feeling very welcomed in our new home church. In fact, God was using this New Hope Church to usher healing in many ways. Yes, His healing forgiveness was washing over us. And we were beginning to see that our family was growing stronger through it all. As difficult as this new frontier was panning out to be, we were growing in our faith, connected together, and our roots were intertwining like those of the mighty redwoods. We were finding golden nuggets of hidden treasure in the truth that we truly are better and stronger together. Opening our hearts to allow His healing forgiveness to flood our wounds and flow through us has made this journey through a valley of pain somehow refreshing.

Restore our fortunes, Lord, as streams renew the desert. Those who plant in tears will harvest with shouts of joy. They weep as they go to plant their seed, but they sing as they return with the harvest. Psalm 126:4–6

Chapter 9

HOPE-VICTORY

Defeated. The twists and turns of this new frontier had me feeling defeated. The season held deep freedom and treasures untold, yet the unseen circumstances were weighing me down. When the raging storm won't quit and the waves kick up to intense levels, your soul can feel defeated. A peace to one storm had come, and our family was enjoying falling into a place of continued soul healing at our new church. Yet there was an undercurrent stirring strong and fierce.

In early 2018, our eleven-year-old son Evan needed to have a variety of tests. What we knew was that after an infection, Evan began having gastrointestinal issues and a bout of severe pain. While his symptoms seemed to have subsided, we still needed to follow up with a GI doctor. The first round of testing showed that Evan's inflammation markers were high and his vitamin D and iron levels were low. Due to the fact that he was fighting a round of the flu, we waited a few weeks and repeated the lab work.

Evan has always been a lover of patterns and order. Change is his mortal enemy. While he doesn't remember his first move from Georgia to New Jersey, it manifested as a struggle for him in his carting of totes. He had these little totes that held his most prized toys: cars, trains, planes, anything with wheels. As I settled in and unpacked throughout the day, he would cart his little totes with him and follow me from room to room. Even when I would go down the hallway to use the bathroom, he would bring his totes and sit in the hallway with them, waiting for me. It was really cute, but I knew as his momma it was his way of dealing with the change. It was a way to help him feel secure. Isn't that something we all long for? To feel secure?

Change obviously came time and again for Evan. While the move from New Jersey to our new frontier of California wasn't easy, he seemed to fall into place quickly, and he wasn't carrying totes everywhere he went. A perfect storm of change was brewing, and the undercurrent started creating waves of severe uncertainty. Evan faced rounds of lab work and a season of the unknown. Due to a variety of circumstances, we were in the process of looking for a new school for Evan and Bella to attend in the fall. We were adjusting to Grandma living with us. I was back and forth a lot as I was overseeing a remodel of my parents' home before its eventual sale. My parents' ongoing health issues became close to home with Grandma under our roof. All of this was a lot for Evan to deal with. I thought maybe his GI issues were just a case of a nervous tummy.

Thankfully, God joins us in the waiting rooms of life, even throwing in fun surprises while we wait. Evan was enjoying playing on a basketball team and having the time of his life. His team spirit and driving effort were fun to watch from the bleachers. One day, we took Evan to tour a potential new school that hosted some of his basketball games. During the tour, he saw one of his teammates and was so excited about the possibility of change. You know God is doing something when your son, who resists change, starts to be excited. And after praying about it, we did feel that God was leading our family to make the move to that exact school. God was showing Evan that even in the midst of the unknown, He was orchestrating things for our good.

The second round of lab work came back, and the test results were the same. Evan, at this point, seemed stable. His tummy wasn't bothering him at all, but the doctor was concerned. On March 8, Evan was put under anesthesia to undergo an upper and lower endoscopy. That same morning, one of my beloved uncles was facing his own health crisis that had him undergoing brain surgery. Evan and my uncle both made it through their procedures successfully, and the waiting began once again. Oh, those dreaded times of waiting. We humans like answers and quick resolutions. The tension of the waiting was pulling strong on our entire family.

At the end of March 2018, Evan and I headed to a follow-up with his GI doctor to review his endoscopy results. We were told that all his biopsy results were normal and there were no food allergies. With Evan stable, we were given the all-clear by the doctor. Evan was so happy. A few weeks later in early April, Evan celebrated his eleventh birthday, and our family spent a week at a cabin in the redwoods of Northern California. It was a fun-filled week of spring break and just the getaway we needed. We played board games and watched movies. Laughter spilled over into our lives, and we were enjoying moments of refreshment.

The school year began to come to a close, and we were looking forward to a summer spent poolside and a visit with John's parents. A few weeks before school was out, Evan missed almost an entire week of school with a touch of a tummy bug. Thankfully, it passed and the rest of us were spared. I am not a fan of the dreaded tummy bug. Then again, I don't know anyone who is. School eventually ended, and the long, lazy days of summer were upon us. Or so I thought.

Summer 2018 was sheer insanity for us. As I mentioned in the last chapter, it was filled with more than its fair share of doctor and hospital visits. The waves seemed to be getting more intense, and yet I would come to find out that this storm had only just begun. The beginning of our summer saw some work travel for my husband, as well as the all-too-soon and unfortunate loss of my beloved uncle. The brain surgery back in March and the ongoing health issues never resolved. His beautiful life entered eternity far sooner than our family desired. Loss weighed heavy, and that feeling of defeat began to press in even more.

Sprinkled into the middle of our summer of insanity was a wonderful visit from John's parents. These Virginia grandparents are loved by us all, and we enjoyed each sweet moment with them. A day trip with them to hike in the redwoods ended up being a highlight of our summer as a family. There were a couple of days during their visit when Evan's tummy began to bother him. I hoped deeply that it was nothing, but my momma heart just knew.

Evan's abdominal cramping and GI issues returned with a vengeance, and by July we were desperate for answers. I kept telling Evan that his biopsies and test results were normal, so whatever it was couldn't be too serious. I was doing my best to keep him, and myself, from worrying. Evan's issues intensified and food was going through him faster than it should have. He started losing weight, and he began to see the doctor frequently. His pediatrician ordered weight checks, blood tests, and even an abdominal x-ray to rule out any potential blockages that could be causing the pain. The pain at times was so intense that Evan would be screaming and the rest of us would be crying and praying as the waves crashed onto the shore of our new frontier.

One afternoon, I was on the phone with the pediatrician, going over lab results and trying to find answers. On a hunch, she pulled up the biopsy results from the spring. While the cover letter from the GI doctor stated that Evan's results were normal, the last page of the biopsy said it loud and clear: "The findings are suggestive of inflammatory bowel diseases." The pathologist recommended treatment for ulcerative colitis by a GI doctor, and all the while we had no clue. The pediatrician apologized from the bottom of her heart. How could we have missed this? At that moment, I didn't blame her. The cover letter said the results were normal. As a busy doctor, I would have probably filed it away in the chart and called it done. As Evan's momma, I never got a copy of those biopsy results, and that afternoon I requested the doctor make a copy for my records. The pediatrician looked up some GI doctors and I made a few phone calls.

Time seemed to slow as I dialed numbers and asked questions. What was happening to my son? How serious was this ulcerative colitis? How was our world going to change? Would Evan be okay? The questions raced through my mind as I spoke with a few doctors trying to find a new gastroenterologist to treat my son ASAP. Thankfully, we found a new GI doctor through UCSF Benioff Children's Hospital in Oakland, who made an opening to see Evan the next day. I made a copy of Evan's biopsy results to bring with us and off we went to UCSF. Evan's new doctor was wonderful. Filled with compassion and a passion for her job, she made us feel like she was on our team and she was committed to walk through this journey with us. Evan felt really comfortable with her, which was very helpful as he was facing a very uncomfortable disease. The doctor prescribed a maintenance medication for ulcerative colitis, along with another round of prednisone to help with the intense inflammation.

In August 2018, Janelle began her sophomore year of high school. Evan entered junior high and Bella started kindergarten at their new school with much excitement. My husband's work had him in England for their first two weeks of school, and I entered into my 40s. The usual school morning rush also came with a new route as Evan and Bella's school was just a bit further away from home. In the summer, I could easily get to their school in twenty minutes, but living in the Bay Area of California, I share the morning commute with millions of people. We had to be out the door one hour and fifteen minutes before school began. The slow-moving traffic became torturous in moments when Evan's tummy would writhe in pain. We were hoping the medications would put his symptoms at bay. We were learning that Evan's body was in a UC flare and that finding the right treatment would take time. Those moments in the car with Evan screaming in pain were heart-wrenching. Bella would often snuggle with her blanket in the car on the long drive. I would often see her head under the blanket as she tried to use it to block out the sound of Evan's screams. Janelle would silently cry and pray, and I would often go into full-out, battle-prayer mode.

"Oh Jesus, bring healing to my son. We need you." Groanings from my spirit cried out in prayer became the norm. We were in the throes of figuring out how to care for Evan. The stress of the morning rush seemed to be intensifying his symptoms, and my heart was just breaking. Evan would cry out, "Jesus, why? Please, Jesus, help me." The emotion rises in me even as I type these words.

The next few months brought more pain-filled mornings and symptoms that seemed to get better once we arrived safely at school. Evan joined the flag football team and miraculously was able to play just about every game of the season. He missed a couple of practices for follow-up doctor visits and ongoing lab work. By mid-October, Evan completed his first tapered dose of prednisone and once again, we entered a season of waiting to see how his body would respond.

A few short weeks went by, and by November 2, 2018, Evan's symptoms were raging so fiercely that he was admitted to the Children's Hospital for an emergency infusion. I found myself packing what would be the first of many hospital overnight bags. I had recently joined the prayer ministry team at our church. That evening, we were having a team meeting, and I found myself on the way to the hospital instead. In desperate need of prayer, I emailed the entire team asking them to cover us. Someone I barely knew reached out immediately. A brother in the faith actually came all the way out to Oakland to visit us and pray for Evan. He even brought a friend. They patiently waited through a very long IV placement process. Evan's body was dehydrated, and in this flare, he was losing not only water but blood as well. With his body in such a weakened state, it took a while to find a good vein for the IV. I couldn't believe my son was having to go through this. I also couldn't believe the unexpected outpouring of love from two new friends who prayed for my son. We were touched beyond words. The family of God was surrounding us. These brothers in the Lord laid their hands on my beloved son and asked the God of all creation to come and bring healing. We hugged them and thanked them with tears in our eyes. And off they went, to drive back home in thick rush-hour traffic. It was the love of Jesus covering us from the moment of admission.

During that first hospital stay, we began to learn how to navigate bathroom trips with an IV pole. Evan became a pro at connecting and disconnecting his heart monitor lines. We ordered hospital food, watched movies, and played card games to pass the time. It was a boot camp of sorts: figuring out how to do life on the inside, how to ignore all the hospital sounds so you can nap, how to deal with the many interruptions to those naps once they finally came, how to keep your spirits up with lots of prayers and reading encouraging portions of the Bible, and how to survive. While we were thankful for this place, it was also a place that was very scary for a child. Evan just wanted to feel better and go home. He wanted the prodding and poking to stop. He was feeling defeated and, similar to his momma, just wanted to see a victory.

That first hospital stay changed the doctor's course of action for treating Evan's UC. Another dose of prednisone was started. The inflammation in Evan's body was very quick to obey the steroids and calm down. However, the steroids made his body carry extra water and he had that round steroid face with puffy cheeks. His emotions were more on edge with the steroids as well, and frustrations ran higher than normal under these abnormal circumstances. Evan's GI team of doctors decided to start him on an infused medication called Remicade. He had his first infusion that weekend, and he began a schedule of infusions that would be needed for life. According to man, there is no cure for ulcerative colitis. Evan chose to believe from the very beginning that God would one day bring healing to his body. As a family, we choose to believe along with him and trust God to lead the doctors as the Great Physician that He is.

After a few days, Evan was stable enough to be released. Getting out of the hospital that first time felt so great, yet we were still facing the great unknown. Evan missed some school here and there due to his battle with UC. Thankfully, his teachers, principal, and the whole school office staff were kind, compassionate, and very understanding. Evan was given time to make up assignments and was able to keep up his workload. We were thankful for the change to this new school. God knew ahead of time the season Evan would be navigating at the start of junior high, and this school couldn't have been a more perfect place for us to land. The downside and a very huge disappointing part of this UC journey was that Evan began to miss out not just on regular school days, but the fun times too—those field trips to science centers, or the theatre production during the holidays, a concert, and even a chance to see the Harlem Globetrotters. To say it was hard is an understatement. Those missing-out moments are all the more difficult when you are the only kid you know facing the great unknown.

Evan gave his ever and always tender heart to Jesus when he was at the tender age of four. This son of mine, who I often refer to as my diamond in the rough, was born with a golden heart of compassion for God and the many people He created. Almost a year prior to the beginning of our hospital visits, Evan voiced to his dad and I that he felt the call on his life to be a pastor. He was a few months shy of turning eleven at the time and his heart was to shepherd the Good Shepherd's people. Now he was facing a battle that would truly put his faith to a test.

By mid-November, Evan had a second infusion of the Remicade, and we prayed it would keep him stable for a surprise we had in store. We did not want him to miss this experience. God answered our prayers, and we were able to take the kids on a surprise experience trip during the week of Thanksgiving as an early Christmas gift. We wanted their Christmas gift to be an experience of memory-making adventures, rather than a tangible gift that would fade with time. As difficult as things were growing up, my parents always overdid the gift-giving at Christmas and birthdays. While I appreciated the gifts, what I really wanted was to spend time as a family. I longed to go on fun family trips and adventures. So I made a decision to offer those experiences to my own children. It was an amazing week. We even took our beloved uncle Gary along with us. Bringing people along in your journey is always fun and has a way of multiplying joy. We loaded the minivan and headed seven hours south to Southern California. We went to Disneyland, Sea World, and the beautiful San Diego Zoo. We walked until we thought our feet would fall off. We had a truly amazing, memory-making trip together, and Evan felt good the entire time. I was so very thankful for those moments together and that, so far, it seemed this new infusion medication was working.

Moments with the people who we love are the best gifts we can give each other. That fact was fresh in our hearts and minds. The month surrounding Thanksgiving, our family experienced the loss of another beloved uncle, as well as two cousins. Each life is so special, so significant, and so irreplaceable. My heart was heavy in a way I had never experienced before. The weight of walking through the valley of the shadow of death all while navigating a disease that would flare up and have my son screaming in pain was just so heavy. Somehow, I kept standing, kept believing for the healing, kept putting one foot in front of the other, hoping for victory in what seemed like a deluge of defeat.

Early December rushed in like a bull as Evan's symptoms returned in full force. On a Sunday after church, he continued to get worse. At this point, I was able to send messages to his GI doctor through an online patient portal. She was always so quick to respond, and I really appreciated that. We arranged for Evan to see her the next day. That evening on my way to pick up Janelle from the youth group, I saw something I had been driving by yet had never noticed: Victory Village. It used to be a Navy housing complex that had been abandoned for many years. It was dilapidated, rundown, and broken. I remember thinking, "How sad, even Victory Village looks defeated." But God started to speak to my heart about living in victory. Here is what I wrote in my journal that night the moment I arrived at church:

In the darkness of night...with the glittering of Christmas on the peripheral...I drive past an abandoned housing complex: victory village....in that moment I hear His whispers: "My beloved, the only way to live in victory is to have won the battle. I fought the ultimate battle on the cross on your behalf. I defeated death, hell, and the grave. I am your victorious King and therefore your truest reality is that you are victorious with me, seated in the heaven-lies. You will always come through any battle victorious as long as you are following me. Even these storms that are raging....each battle you find yourself in right now, we will be victorious together. Stand strong, pray hard, praise even harder, and know that even though it looks like you are surrounded, the truth is you are surrounded by my presence. No weapon formed against you will prosper. No gate of hell can prevail against you. Your faith shield is putting out every single fiery dart of the enemy. You are my beloved warrior bride, and I am pleased and delighted in you. Come now and feast at the table I have prepared for you in the presence of your enemies... there is nothing like feasting at this table with me, and you can only feast here in the midst of battle. Enjoy all I am nourishing your spirit with."

You prepare a feast for me in the presence of my enemies. Psalm 23:5a

132

Jesus is always so faithful to speak to my heart when I need to hear Him the most. I wept as I wrote down the revelation He gave me. I sang spontaneously in worship to the King who won the victory for me. I didn't know how He would do it, but I knew that together we would win this battle. One thing I did know was that his directive to praise even harder compelled me to do just that. I knew He was telling me that there was a weapon in my praise, a weapon in my song.

The LORD is my strength and my song; he has given me victory.
Psalm 118:14

The Lord is my strength and shield. I trust him with all my heart.
He helps me, and my heart is filled with joy. I burst out in songs of
thanksgiving. Psalm 28:7

See, God has come to save me. I will trust in him and not be afraid.
The Lord God is my strength and my song; he has given me victory.
Isaiah 12:2

Because Jesus is victorious on our behalf and because He fights for us, we can be still under His protection. In the shadows of our waiting times, we can sing for joy. Oh, beloved, I was learning that the King who reigns victorious longs for His joy to be our strength in the battle. He longs for us to know that He died and rose again to position us for victory.

For the joy of the Lord is your strength! Nehemiah 8:10

That Monday afternoon, Evan was admitted to the hospital again for an overnight stay and another emergency infusion. We were told the Remicade would take a while to build up in the body. We were told that it would be at least three months from that first infusion to know if it was actually working to keep Evan's UC under control. The long-term goal was remission, but we were nowhere near that stage. This full-on flare had our son screaming in pain yet again. That night was horrible. The doctors recommended a new medication: Methotrexate, a low dose of chemo medication. When paired with the Remicade, it can help to get symptoms under control. It was something the doctors mentioned before as a possibility, and my momma heart was totally against it. Evan was already on some strong medication with potential side effects that were indeed worrisome. For some reason, I just wanted to scream, "No," to adding another medication into the mix.

After some lengthy conversations, and prayer, we made the decision to try adding the Methotrexate. One thing we were learning about hospital admissions and emergency infusions is that they take time. Time in hospitals passes by so very slowly. With the decision made, John decided he would stay with Evan for the night and I headed home. About an hour after his first dose of Methotrexate, Evan experienced extreme pain and discomfort. He was sick nonstop for over an hour, and John was beside himself. My heart sank the next morning when I heard his voice on the phone. He sounded just like I felt: defeated.

All I could think was, "Okay Jesus, I'm ready for you to ride in on that white horse and declare victory over this ulcerative colitis. You said we would be victorious, and I am ready. Bring it!" Maybe I was more demanding than praying at that moment. I hated knowing that Evan had such a horrible night. The doctors reassured us that the medication was not the reason for his symptoms. I was just unsure, and so we held off on continuing the Methotrexate. Evan was stable enough the next evening to come home. I was beginning to see those homecomings as mini-victories in the midst of the battle.

Christmas and New Year's came and went with a mostly stable break from school. We enjoyed time together as a family staying close to home. We all longed for a fresh start as the New Year of 2019 arrived. While we sensed the excitement of a new year and new possibilities, there was also that great unknown of which we were in the middle that continued to weigh heavily. Ten days into the new year and Evan was back at the hospital again. At this point, he should have been able to go four weeks between his infusions and he had yet to make it that far. Another quick overnight stay and he would be infused and released to come back home. This time, though, he would only be stable for a few days before his body raged in pain again in an ongoing flare. This new year was turning out to not be a fresh start at all.

Evan would spend six days in the hospital. We were becoming hospital-fatigued at this point. The night he was admitted would also be the night of another blow of bad news. A lifelong friend of mine just found out she had cancer. On January 18, Evan's doctors decided to do a colonoscopy to see if his UC spread any further into his GI tract. That same morning, while I was waiting for my son to wake up from anesthesia, I was also waiting on a call from my dear friend's husband with an update. The waiting room was filled with other parents of children who were facing their own great unknown. We all waited in silence. Eventually, my friend's husband would text me with the news that the full hysterectomy went smoothly, and they believed they got all the cancer out. Tears of relief flooded down my face. Then Evan's medical team came to get me. I stepped into the hallway and lost it. The weight of it all crumbled my entire being. I fell into the arms of one of the doctors who just let me cry and reassured me that Evan was fine. I told them quickly about the news of my dear friend and they were speechless.

I remember that sweet medical team being filled with com-passion for what I was facing. A friend with cancer, a son whose flaring UC wouldn't quit, and three recent losses in our family. It was just too much to bear, and yet I stood there and told them that I knew Jesus would give me the strength to keep going through the storm. They listened to me, encouraged me, and with other patients waiting, eventually they brought the conversation back to my son and the update on their findings. The UC had indeed spread farther into his GI tract, yet it was still contained in the large intestine. Once it travels farther than the large intestine, it would be diagnosed as Crohn's disease. UC was bad enough; we did not want this turning into Crohn's. The medical team, at this point, was kind of split on what to do for Evan's continuing treatment. I am thankful that the team discussed Evan's case together, allowed us time to ask many questions, and gave Evan a few days to just recover and stabilize. Eventually, we decided to add Methotrexate to see if that would be the kick the Remicade and Evan's body needed to stop this intense flare. Another round of prednisone was in order. As well, a variety of other medications were put into his weekly regimen to aid in the relief of some side effects like heartburn, as well as help support his compromised immune system.

Six long days in the hospital felt like too much. Evan seemed pretty down and defeated. I didn't want him to feel defeated. I wanted to feel that for him. I'd take a double or triple portion of feeling defeated if it would help protect his heart from the crushing of this great unknown. This heart-wrenching hospital stay opened our eyes to the suffering around us in new ways. There were various activities for the children to participate in during the week. There was a classroom where we could sit and get some homework done. We had fun learning origami from a hospital volunteer and met some other children while doing that. There were children that were much sicker than Evan, which was heartbreaking—children with cancer and various diseases, children who were wheelchair-bound, or children who had a halo in place around their head to keep their spine aligned after reconstructive surgery. The despair was so thick you could cut it with a knife, and yet there was a childlike joy that sparkled out and bubbled up here and there in simple ways, like when we were folding little paper animals or playing bingo on a Thursday night.

One young girl, in particular, stood out to us. It was the one with the halo. I don't know all that she was facing, but we were drawn to her. I made her laugh a few times during the origami session, and we ended up seeing her later that week for bingo night. She sat right next to me, and we laughed through every round. Somehow, God was using me to bring joy to this young girl. The evening of bingo ended, and the kids took turns selecting their prizes. Our new friend thanked me over and over for making her laugh so much. She put her hand on mine and asked me, "Would you play bingo with me next Thursday night?" I looked into her eyes and said, "I don't know if I will be here next Thursday, but if I am, I'd love nothing more than to sit next to you for bingo night and laugh all over again." The hope in her eyes at the possibility of me being there literally broke me inside.

As soon as we had entered the hospital, we were ready to go home. Evan became nervous about IV placement and was just uncomfortable from the moment he got to admissions. No child wants to be in the hospital. This young girl had been there for weeks, and for all I knew, she had weeks to go before they would release her to go home. At that moment, I just wanted to run away and cry into a pillow somewhere. I took slow, deep breaths trusting that God would give me the strength to get through even this. After Evan selected his prizes, we stepped into the hallway to head back to his room. Then Evan's dam broke and the tears flowed freely. When we got back to his room, we just held each other and cried a good, long cry. None of this was easy for Evan, but what tore him up the most was seeing other kids going through their great unknowns. His heart of compassion for others was breaking and expanding to a new capacity. His heart of compassion was actually enlarging, and it was beautiful to see. We prayed for all the children in that hospital, and he was determined to color a card with a Bible verse on it to give to our new friend. The day we were discharged, we asked around to see if the nurses knew who we were trying to find. We never did catch her name, and Evan was determined to bless this girl before we went home. The pastor's heart God was forming in him was on display and it was breathtaking. God eventually led us to the right floor, and we found our friend. She was so appreciative that we gave her something. We told her we would pray for her and said our goodbyes.

Evan and I walked back out into the great unknown determined to win this UC battle. Evan also determined that when that day arrived, he would be back at the hospital volunteering to play bingo with children on Thursday nights if they would let him. What we were facing paled in comparison to so many other children who were spending much more time on the inside than we were. How I longed to see them all receive a healing touch. How I longed for my own son's healing. Evan determined to go forward for prayer at church every Sunday until God brought that healing.

Evan was taking so much medication. From the start, we prayed over him before every infusion, as well as when he would take his morning and evening meds. We prayed that the medications would only benefit Evan and that there would be no negative side effects. We started sharing communion together each night, believing that Jesus paid for Evan's healing. In faith, we told his GI tract that it was under the stripes of Jesus who paid for our healing. We were believing with Evan for his complete and total healing. And we continued to wait.

One of the treatments that the doctors suggested was so very painful to administer to Evan. He screamed and cried in pain as I helped administer the first dose. I cried right along with him and just kept saying the name of Jesus over and over. The next night, I had to administer another dose. I prayed all day that God would help us both and especially help Evan to remain calm and have the strength to endure the pain. With tears in our eyes, I began administering the medication. Evan, through the tears and pain, declared over and over, "I praise you, Jesus. I praise you, Jesus." It was heart-wrenching and beautiful all wrapped in a horrific moment of time. Evan was praising Jesus in the midst of his very real and intense storm. His faith was not shaken, and he was thankful that Jesus was right there inside of him, giving him the strength to carry on. The lessons he was learning in the middle of this storm were refining his faith. His body may have been weak, but his spirit was getting stronger.

Meanwhile, my dad was back in the hospital again and my mom was having increasing doctor visits. My dad's health started to decline in the early part of 2019, and we were seeing more and more doctors. His legs became very weak and his ability to stand and have me assist him in transfers from the wheelchair to the car and back were quickly fading. I started researching possible transportation options for him, while also juggling the many doctor visits for Evan and my mom. Bella and Evan both ended up breaking bones, so that added a handful of doctor visits to our already full calendar. I was beginning to feel like a medical chauffeur, yet no one was paying me. It was a very draining season. I longed for a break and some downtime, and yet the word God had given me for the year was Accelerate. I hoped it meant that things would rapidly change for the better. My flesh feared it meant an insane intensification of all things pertaining to my life. Maybe that fear was really just a revelation from the Lord because the year started off with an acceleration of just about everything. I referred to life as the whirlwind, and Jesus was showing me more and more that in the middle of all of this, I was just dancing on the waves with Him.

By mid-March 2019, Evan ended another dose of prednisone and in less than a month's time, he was back to full-flare mode. We were facing another hospital admission, another round of prednisone, another emergency infusion, and another round of in-depth conversations with the GI team of doctors caring for our son. Through some waiting and testing, we soon found out that Evan's UC was not responding to the Remicade. I felt like the last five months had been a waste of time—like we were using meds on my son as some kind of science experiment and it brought only torture. Our family was broken for our sweet Evan. Seeing him in so much pain, hearing his cries and his desperate prayers were more than we could bear. Somehow, by the grace of God, Jesus held us together and we prayed more than ever before. I posted scriptures all throughout the house to remind Evan that Jesus was fighting this battle for him. That he was more than a conqueror and that he could be brave and courageous as he trusted in the Lord.

The Lord himself will fight for you. Just stay calm. Exodus 14:14

But God is my helper. The Lord keeps me alive! Psalm 54:4

I wait quietly before God, for my victory comes from him. He alone is my rock and my salvation, my fortress where I will never be shaken. Psalm 62:1–2

Wait patiently for the Lord. Be brave and courageous. Yes, wait patiently for the Lord. Psalm 27:14

The angel of the Lord encamps around those who fear him, and he delivers them. Psalm 34:7 NIV

In the middle of feeling defeated, God was placing His truth right before our very eyes. He was not only the Lord of the battle, but He was in the battle fighting on our behalf—fighting for my son, fighting for my parents, and fighting for my lifelong friend who turned out to actually be fighting stage four colon cancer. The season was pressing and crushing in ways you can only know if you go through it yourself. What I did know is that God was holding us together, and He was showing me that a person is not defined by their disease. We are defined by the great Creator God who formed us in our mother's womb. The focus wasn't the stage of our disease, it was the stage of our life, and He is faithful to take center stage and be the Famous One, fighting on our behalf even when we don't see it. He even gave me an acronym for my friend and others who I would come to know who are fighting their own battle against cancer. CHEMO stands for Christ Healing Every Malignant Organism. I began declaring that over friends and loved ones who were facing this oftentimes violent and toxic treatment. It turned out that my son's faith wasn't the only thing being forged by the fires of this battle.

At some point in April, Evan's GI medical team agreed, as did we, that it was time to switch to a new medication for his infusion treatment. On May 2, 2019, Evan had his first treatment of Entyvio. He also started an almost four-month-long tapered dose of prednisone as his body adjusted to the new medication. You see, it's not that my son was a science experiment, but these treatments take time to work. While it felt like the battle would just be drug out even longer, our son was worth the risk and the wait. We continued to feel the weight of the battle as we waited. The school year came to an end, and Evan managed to keep a 4.0 and be the top student of his sixth-grade class—an amazing feat for all he was facing as well as being at a new school. We couldn't have been prouder.

We stepped into another summer, and we were hopeful that this new treatment would work. Filled with the peace of Jesus that not only passes all understanding but became this protecting peace that overwhelmed us in the best of ways, we flew to Virginia to visit grandparents, cousins, and a host of family and friends. We spent a few glorious days in Emerald Isle, North Carolina, enjoying the waves, the aquarium, and seeing firsthand an island that was rising back up in restoration after their own very intense storm that hit months prior. We saw a glorious, full rainbow stretched out over the open ocean that lasted for almost half an hour. It was one of those God-wink kinds of moments. In the middle of this battle, He was reminding us of His promise in the sky. Our entire three weeks of vacation were also filled with another great unknown. My dad went to the hospital with a case of sepsis and miraculously came back from the brink of death. There were a few moments when I had to make the decision if I would stay in Virginia on vacation with my family or fly back home to possibly say goodbye to my dad. God answered our prayers, and he made a full recovery but spent almost two months in the hospital and skilled nursing rehabilitation facilities.

Evan was stable for our entire vacation, and it felt like a possible silver lining. My dad was on the mend and God opened up an opportunity for us to move him to a new board-and-care home just five minutes from our house. It felt like a new season was starting to break in. By August 2019, school was starting again, and Evan was coming off his crazy months-long dose of prednisone. I continued to spend days chauffeuring family to various doctor visits. I even stepped into a leadership role at church on our prayer ministry team and was coming alive in ways I never dreamed. God was encouraging me and He was using me as I would freely share that encouragement with others. I was ever-treasuring the honor and joy to pray for others and stand with them in the midst of their own battles. All the while, I was learning a thing or two.

Jesus was showing me a new level of trusting in Him. A picture came to my mind during a worship moment yet again. A little girl looked up into the eyes of Jesus, who was the full representation of the Father God. Her hands were extended up to Him in surrender and trust, and at the same time her little hands were holding tightly to his. Her little feet in black dress shoes were standing right on top of his. They were on top of the waves, in the dark of night, dancing over the storm under both stars and moonlight. You see, beloved, Jesus wants us to be filled with that kind of faith—like a little child, secure on her Father's feet, allowing Him to dance her over the waves of life, looking intently into His eyes, acknowledging the storm on the peripheral, but never letting her eyes off His and facing Him in the midst of her circumstances.

Between July 30 and September 30, Evan successfully came off of four medications, including the dreaded prednisone, with no return of symptoms. On October 16, 2019, Evan's GI doctor gave us the most amazing news. A declaration of *remission*! Evan's Calprotectin number was down to twenty-two. At the height of his UC flare, his lab results were over 1,250. The normal range is between ten and sixty. That news, in and of itself, was a miracle for us. Entyvio was working. Evan gained weight and grew in height at a healthy pace. He was feeling great and looking so very good. The tears of joy brought such relief and the weight of the battle lessoned. The year continued on with some very close calls for my mom, as she spent four separate short stays in the hospital. A diagnosis of congestive heart failure made staying healthy all the more tricky. At the end of December, a diagnosis of AFIB required that her heart be shocked back into a normal rhythm.

With all of our issues, 2019 was another year for the record books. Our family had 206 doctor and hospital visits for the year. That is over half a year's worth of days spent dealing with health issues. In the thickness of the battle, we had moments of feeling defeated more often than not. However, Jesus died so that we could be positioned for victory, and that truth held us together, giving us the strength to stand.

Every tough circumstance or storm we face is an opportunity for us to grow in our faith and trust Jesus more deeply. It is also an opportunity for the enemy to take advantage. These are the moments when the enemy of our soul doesn't lie in wait—he straight-up lies to us while we are waiting for God to move. We must know that there is an epic battle for our soul's allegiance. Jesus proved His great love for us on the cross and the enemy steps into every scene trying his best in the worst way to get us to question that great love, to question the hope of victory for which we are positioned in Christ. This kingdom of God is a kingdom built on humility, so it's often hard for us to see God moving. The enemy is filled with pride, and he desires nothing more than to puff up with lies right to our face. BUT GOD! God is faithful to His love and His promises. He quietly pursues us through both stormy and calm seasons. We must be looking for Him and seeking Him. And we can be assured that there is a reward for those who seek Him. It is true that Jesus prepares a table for us in the midst of our battle. He is also preparing a banquet table in glory for us. As His followers, indeed as His bride, we are positioned for that victory at His table.

It will be good for those servants whose master finds them watching when he comes. Truly I tell you, he will dress himself to serve, will have them recline at the table and will come and wait on them.
Luke 12:37 NIV

He will wipe all tears from their eyes, and there will be no more death, suffering, crying, or pain. These things of the past are gone forever.
Revelation 21:4 CEV

The Lord is my strength and my song; he has given me victory.
Exodus 15:2a

We haven't yet heard Evan's medical team say the words *miracle* or *healing*, but we believe it's possible. We haven't yet seen complete healing for our friend facing cancer, but we believe it's possible. That is the kind of God we serve—the One who sees unlimited possibilities, the One who is planning a great restoration of all things, and the One who has streets of gold in glory planned for all those who put their trusting faith in His son Jesus. I wanted to wait to finish this book once we experienced the fullness of Evan's miracle and that declaration of healing from his doctors. However, I know His voice is saying it's time to end this chapter and begin an ending to this book. There is a great mystery to God. He is sovereign overall, and His deepest desire is that we would trust and love Him with all that we are.

Will you place your hands up in surrender to Him? Will you hold onto Him tightly? Will you fix your eyes on his? Will you place your feet securely on His and allow Him to dance you over the waves of your life's circumstances? Will you trust in the rainbow of His promises that are chasing after you with all His heart and believe His truth over the lies of the evil one? Will you join me, beloved, in this great beauty of hope dance? It will be worth it, so very worth it. We can dance on as we hope in His victory. And we can be sure that one day we will take a step in this dance and He will graciously sway us over the waves onto His glorious streets of gold. Beloved, we will see the victory!

But thank God! He gives us victory over sin and death through our Lord Jesus Christ. 1 Corinthians 15:57

BEGINNING ENDINGS

Endings always feel bittersweet this side of glory. What is utterly true is that an ending is just the beginning. The best is always yet to come, and our best days are always before us in Christ. Living in the eternal Kingdom of God begins when our lives end. Not when our physical body passes away, but when we give our lives to Jesus and begin a relationship with Him. Our lives become his.

My old self has been crucified with Christ. It is no longer I who live, but Christ lives in me. So I live in this earthly body by trusting in the Son of God, who loved me and gave himself for me. Galatians 2:20

This eternal life begins, and we see Him transforming us into His image, from glory to glory by the Spirit of the Lord. Jesus told us we would face trouble in this world. We will indeed face the great unknowns of this new life in Christ. However, we can be sure that Jesus is faithful to turn even the worst of things we face into good. With Jesus every ending is a beginning.

And we know that God causes everything to work together for the good of those who love God and are called according to his purpose for them. Romans 8:28

I have always loved stories. The most treasured adventures will have us on the edge of our seats as we consume every word with our eyes, sometimes bloodshot from staying up too late to see how the story ends. I have also always been a planner who loves the details and specifics. While I love the adventure of a good book, it has been a process for me to learn to live like the Bible tells us Jesus lived. He was obedient to the Father and obeyed no matter what the cost. Jesus, God's own Son, the Word made flesh, walked on shore and on the waves in the adventure of a lifetime—all the while praying. His connection to the Father and the Holy Spirit was so intimate. The Three-in-One God in flesh, intertwined together walking upon the earth they created. I believe that Jesus was led by the Father through those intimate times of prayer. His ultimate model prayer shows us that His heart's desire was for the will of God to be done. He was obedient and willing to follow the leading of the Holy Spirit and the Father as He journeyed through time. It's taken me a long time to be comfortable with following that kind of leading.

But Jesus often withdrew to lonely places and prayed. Luke 5:16 NIV

Your kingdom come, your will be done, on earth as it is in heaven.
Matthew 6:10 NIV

I am not sure about you, but oftentimes I think it would be much easier to have the whole story written out for me, like a playbook of sorts. I want the direction and specifics of what will happen next so I don't have to worry about what may happen. John Wimber once said, "Faith is spelled R-I-S-K." This life of faith is truly that. Risking it all in obedience, not knowing what may come. We live in faith, anchored by hope, and compelled to carry on by the hope that is to come. We may know the end of the story because the Bible tells us of that coming glory. Yet Jesus calls us to faith in Him, a faith in the unseen.

Now faith is confidence in what we hope for and assurance about what we do not see. Hebrews 11:1 NIV

This hope is a strong and trustworthy anchor for our souls. It leads us through the curtain into God's inner sanctuary. Romans 6:19

As a momma, I often encourage my own children to follow Jesus where He leads. The more I have trusted His leading, the more I have seen how trustworthy He is in leading. It is then all the easier to trust Him as I step forward in the great unknown journey this side of glory. I've told my children that following Jesus can be likened to signing a blank page agreement. Jesus wants our faith in Him to be a forever yes to whatever He wills. When we give our lives to Him, signing that blank page, He is faithful to fill in the details in His perfect timing. Jesus the Lamb of God is the GAOAT—Greatest Author Of All Time. He has good plans in store for us, even when we cannot see. And we can trust Him to finish the story He is writing in and through our lives.

When I long for that blank page to be filled in with details before I sign it, I think of Abram. Abram was actually given a lot of specifics about what God was getting ready to do through his life. God was promising him a number of descendants that would match the number of the very stars above him. After some clear visions from the Lord, Abram falls asleep and more specifics are revealed.

As the sun was going down, Abram fell into a deep sleep, and a terrifying darkness came down over him. Then the Lord said to Abram, "You can be sure that your descendants will be strangers in a foreign land, where they will be oppressed as slaves for 400 years. But I will punish the nation that enslaves them, and in the end they will come away with great wealth. (As for you, you will die in peace and be buried at a ripe old age.) After four generations your descendants will return here to this land, for the sins of the Amorites do not yet warrant their destruction." Genesis 15:12–16 NIV

Uh, um. Cue the throat clearing. WHAT? Are you even reading this? Go back for a moment and read that passage one more time. Details and specifics in a dream are revealed. The Lord of Heaven and earth allows His faith-filled servant to fall into a deep sleep. A TERRIFYING DARKNESS is allowed to come over him and the specifics are written before his blank page through a dream. After reading that, I am not sure if I would sign the paper. Y'all, the specifics get REAL. Those promised descendants will be equal to the total of a universe of stars. In the end, a promise of great wealth is foretold. However, right in between those amazing promises, the terrifying darkness is revealed. These promised descendants faced 400 years of oppression in slavery.

Okay, now I am conflicted. I thought knowing the details and specifics would be great. It's not often that God gives man such a detailed picture of his future. Would I have said yes as Abram did? Would I have had the faith to believe for the promised precious ones and signed yes to 400 years of slavery? Abram's faith here is amazing. Given the specifics, I am not sure my faith would reflect his. Maybe this blank page way of following Jesus is better. Giving Him my forever "yes" by allowing Him to unveil His plan slowly over the moments of my life, seeing it play out in real-time. And the reality is, beloved, that He alone promises to step into that reality with us. We will never face our circumstances alone.

While I am not sure I would have said yes to that much pain being inflicted on my promised descendants, I am sure of one thing. As I look back over the many testimonies in this book, I would go through all of the painful moments all over again. God has taught me so many valuable lessons about Himself and who I am in Him through everything I've faced. The terrifying darkness of the great unknown is worth it because those I love are worth it—because

Jesus is worth it. He allowed Himself to display a life filled with the beauty of hope, and that is just the kind of life I would say yes to time and time again.

Toward the end of the Bible, we see Abram, now called Abraham, and his wife, Sarah, listed in what is often referred to as the "Faith Hall of Fame."

It was by faith that Abraham obeyed when God called him to leave home and go to another land that God would give him as his inheritance. He went without knowing where he was going. It was by faith that even Sarah was able to have a child, though she was barren and was too old. She believed that God would keep his promise. And so a whole nation came from this one man who was as good as dead—a nation with so many people that, like the stars in the sky and the sand on the seashore, there is no way to count them. All these people died still believing what God had promised them. They did not receive what was promised, but they saw it all from a distance and welcomed it. They agreed that they were foreigners and nomads here on earth. Obviously, people who say such things are looking forward to a country they can call their own. If they had longed for the country they came from, they could have gone back. But they were looking for a better place, a heavenly homeland. That is why God is not ashamed to be called their God, for he has prepared a city for them. Hebrews 11:8,11-16

WOW. The beauty of the hope on display in the Bible. There is a city that God is preparing for us. That unseen faith journey will be worth it in the end. If we are faithful to Him and endure to the end, the Good Book even promises that Jesus will give a new name to each of His beloved faithful ones.

Anyone with ears to hear must listen to the Spirit and understand what he is saying to the churches. To everyone who is victorious I will

give some of the manna that has been hidden away in heaven. And I will give to each one a white stone, and on the stone will be engraved a new name that no one understands except the one who receives it.
Revelation 2:17

I have heard it said that taking the road less traveled is what makes all the difference. When I gave my heart to the Lord at the tender age of five, I had no idea what this walk with Jesus, this road I travel, this journey called life would look like. Turns out there are many views and many times when you are walking in darkness and longing for vision. Webster and his dictionary tell us that a journey is a passage of progress from one state to another, usually like taking a rather long time! Seems it truly takes a lifetime. My travels have taken me through deep valleys and over steep mountains—both lower and higher than I could have imagined.

The lessons learned are treasured and have made my heart stronger. Majestic trees at times have cast a shadow on the path, yet I know that my steps here have been sacred and that He walks with me—I am never alone. It's an adventure filled with storms and rainbows. Jesus has been that peace in my troubled seas, and He chases me with rainbows—his faithful promises. I have had pain on the mountaintop and joy in the valley. At times on my journey through the dark forest when it seems all hope is lost, God will allow me to soar as an eagle above the dark and winding path, above the trees, to restore in me the hope of the dream He has placed in my heart. He will grant me a vision of His hope that both anchors me and sets me free. As I have walked along the shore of His graces, endless waves of grace have washed my feet. He has carried me at times, leaving only His footprints to be seen. I have climbed the rocks of many mountains. When it seemed I was at the end of my rope, I was reminded that this climb to heaven means I am anchored to Jesus and His rope never runs out. He renews my strength, and His strength has been made perfect in my weakness. He has cared for me in the wilderness and made rivers in my driest of desert places.

I often thought this journey was about me, about who I was becoming, the challenges I was overcoming, and the faith I was gaining. This journey is about Him. It's a coming to life of His word in the adventure of life. All I have faced has taught me more of who He is, and I am ever thankful. Though I know not where the journey will take me next, I know *who* goes with me—the God of angel armies. I will journey on, adventure on, and yes, I will walk on with God, for He is making all things new. He is bringing glory and grace out of my trials and fears. He is using all things for my good. He knows His plans for me, and they are for blessing and not harm, always bringing future and hope. With each step I take, I am covered by Him, for His banner over me is love. My heart will forever sing that I am my Beloved's and He is mine. I will journey on, for my stay here is temporary and heaven is my home. And one glorious day, I will dance with Him over the waves into glory onto those streets of gold. This is my story, yes, my testimony. This is the beginning ending. This is the Beauty of Hope.

We can rejoice, too, when we run into problems and trials, for we know that they help us develop endurance. And endurance develops strength of character, and character strengthens our confident hope of salvation. And this hope will not lead to disappointment. For we know how dearly God loves us, because he has given us the Holy Spirit to fill our hearts with his love. Romans 5:3–5

Now may God, the inspiration and fountain of hope, fill you to over-flowing with uncontainable joy and perfect peace as you trust in him. And may the power of the Holy Spirit continually surround your life with his super-abundance until you radiate with hope! Romans 15:13 TPT

Anchored in
the Beloved

Do you know Jesus as your personal Lord and Savior? I invite you to invite Him in. Begin a new life with Jesus today in the beauty of hope, anchored in the Beloved.

As the Scriptures say, No one is righteous—not even one. Romans 3:10

For everyone has sinned; we all fall short of God's glorious standard. Romans 3:23

For the wages of sin is death, but the free gift of God is eternal life through Christ Jesus our Lord. Romans 6:23

But God showed his great love for us by sending Christ to die for us while we were still sinners. Romans 5:8

If you openly declare that Jesus is Lord and believe in your heart that God raised him from the dead, you will be saved. Romans 10:9

So now there is no condemnation for those who belong to Christ Jesus. Romans 8:1

Inviting Jesus into your life is as easy as having a conversation; that is what prayer is.

Dear Jesus, I come to you and acknowledge that I am a sinner. I confess the many ways that I have not followed your standard. Thank you, Jesus, for dying on the cross to pay the price for my sins. Thank you for raising from the dead so I can have eternal life. Thank you for your great love. I declare that you are now my Lord and Savior. I give you my eternal "YES," and thank you for saving me. I ask that you would guide me by your Holy Spirit into all truth. Help me to know you as I read your Bible. I thank you that your banner over me is love. Guide me and teach me how to be anchored in you, Jesus, the Beloved. You are mine and I am yours. In Jesus's name, amen.

If you just prayed that prayer for either the first time or as a re-commitment, let me be the first one to say, "Welcome home." As you begin your journey with Jesus, I want you to know that the true beauty of hope is Jesus, the hope of the world.

And his name will be the hope of all the world. Matthew 12:21

Jesus is your hope and your anchor. Just as the anchor on a ship needs to be raised and lowered by someone on board, we have to put our hands on the anchor of this ship called life. There will be times when we need to encourage ourselves in the Lord. Jesus is Lord and He is the Word made flesh. So encourage yourself with His Word, the Bible. When an attack on your hope invades, let that anchor go ever deeper into Jesus and His promises. You will find His true Word promises to remind your soul of whose you are and who He has positioned you to be.

Why am I discouraged? Why is my heart so sad? I will put my hope in God! I will praise him again—my Savior and my God! Psalm 42:11

Quiet your heart in His presence and pray; keep hope alive as you long for God to come through for you. Psalm 37:7 TPT

This is why I wait upon you, expecting your breakthrough, for your word brings me hope. Psalm 130:5 TPT

I pray that Jesus will guide you to a healthy church where you can grow in your faith. I pray that you will find a small group of believers with whom to walk this faith journey. I pray that the good, good Father will bless you beyond measure with all you need for life and godliness. And I pray that the Holy Spirit will fill you to overflowing through the Beauty of Hope.

WORKS CITED

Allen, Jenny. IF:Gathering, 2015.

IF:Gathering. "Our Vision." Accessed September 12, 2020. https://www.ifgathering.com/our-vision/.

Newton, John. *Amazing Grace*. 1772.

Paul, Marla. "Radiant Zinc Fireworks Reveal Quality of Human Egg." Published April 26, 2016. https://news.northwestern.edu/stories/2016/04/radiant-zinc-fireworks-reveal-quality-of-human-egg.

Voskamp, Ann. "A North American Lent." Published February 2014. http://www.aholyexperience.com/2014/02/a-north-american-lent-when-you-want-to-have-an-appetite-for-god/.